RSEMENTS

Some books do more than merely communicate information—they impart fresh perspective. Candice Smithyman's *Angels of Fire* is one of those books that will change your perspective permanently. You will begin to see the world as the Bible describes it—a place where unseen angelic agents interact with our daily lives in extraordinary ways. Jesus told us that angelic activity would play a critical role in the last days (see Matt. 13:39-41). More than ever, we need our eyes opened to the spiritual world and its activity. You will be filled with joy and awe as you discover what the Bible says about angels and their earthly assignments in *Angels of Fire*.

DANIEL KOLENDA
President of Christ for all Nations

You've got to get your hands on *Angels of Fire*! In it I've learned things about creating an environment that literally invites angels to come and change the atmosphere in my room, in my home, and wherever I go. Hey, why has no one ever told me this before? This is a book you can actually use. When you get this book, if I were you, I'd get one for a friend too. They'll thank you for it, that I promise!

STEVE SHULTZ
The Elijah List

Psalm 104:4 (NKJV) declares, *"Who makes His angels spirits, His ministers a flame of fire"* speaking of the supernatural realm of angels engaged in the affairs of the believers. In this prophetic, revelatory book, *Angels of Fire*, Dr. Candice Smithyman shares sound, uncanny biblical truth, insight, and understanding about these ministering spirits—called angels. From Genesis through Revelation, the Word of God is filled with examples of ordinary men and women having extraordinary angelic encounters, visitations, and assistance—Abraham, Jacob, Daniel, Mary, John, and even Jesus Himself were all visited or assisted by God's unseen messengers and warriors. In Dr. Smithyman's book, you will discover how to partner with your invisible friends to see revival, breakthrough, healing, restoration, and deliverance in your life. But most of all witness salvation come to those called to inherit the kingdom of God! The world is curious about angels! The church needs to acquaint, activate, and partner with them! Angels are more than invisible guardians that perform God's bidding; they are deployed to help usher in one of the greatest moves of God in human history. I highly recommend this powerful book to anyone ready to experience the heavenly reinforcement of angels to your rescue here and now on earth! *Angels of Fire* is a must-read and definitely a game-changer!

DR. HAKEEM COLLINS
Prophetic voice, International speaker
Bestselling author of *Unseen Warfare*

Candice Smithyman walks in the supernatural on a daily basis, and she wants to mentor you to do the same!

As I read this book, it opened my eyes to understand the realm of the supernatural that is all around me. Jesus died so that the veil could be torn and that we can have access to His Throne Room and walk in the supernatural every day.

In this book, you will also learn that God created angels to partner with us to see His plans come to pass on the earth.

I know that as you read this book, your eyes will be opened to realm of the supernatural and your faith will soar!

JACKIE DUVALL
Associate Producer
Sid Roth's *It's Supernatural!*

Dr. Candice Smithyman is a friend who had interviewed me on her *Glory Road* television program. During my encounter with COVID-19, she prayed for fire angels to come heal me and help my immune system. That night as I drifted to sleep, I felt heat in the bottom of my feet that went up my whole body, bringing peace and soothing comfort. I woke up four hours later feeling good for the first time in 18 days! That began my recovery and brought me back from the brink!

STEVE HEMPHILL
Author/Speaker/Teacher
My Search for the Real Heaven, My Search for Prayers Satan Hates, What Are the Stakes?, and *God's Power for Our Daily Battles*
Active-Faith.org

What an insightful book! Candice Smithyman explains how the book is not a theological one but an experiential one. As I read through the pages, I kept referring to the different scriptures that I knew she pulled her statements from. It's definitely an experience, and an anointed one. I'll add that her book is also a theological one too. Read the book and get one for your friends.

JENNIFER EIVAZ
Founder, Harvest International Ministries
Author, *Seeing the Supernatural* and *Prophetic Secrets*

I absolutely love Candice Smithyman's latest book *Angels of Fire.* Most people are not aware of the amazing world of angels that

God gave us. This book will give you strategic insight into angels needed for this season and how to interact with them. I encountered an angel of fire in South Africa in 2009 and it changed my ministry forever. You will love this book—a must-read for this season.

DOUG ADDISON
DougAddison.com
Author of *Hearing God Every Day, Daily Prophetic Words*,
Spirit Connection Podcast, and Prophetic Blog

Dr. Candice Smithyman has done an exceptional job in her smashing revelatory book *Angels of Fire*. This book has immediately become one of my favorites on the subject of angels. She has provided an excellent exposition of scriptures and experiential encounters with the agents of heaven, inviting believers into understanding the realm of the angelic, its operations, and how we learn to partner with God's angelic forces to accelerate supernatural healing, breakthrough, deliverance, miracles, and ultimately the glory of God on earth.

Dr. Candice is an apostolic voice and prophet who has supernatural encounters in ministering with angels to manifest heaven on earth and releasing God's communicative power through His invisible messengers. I highly regard, recommend, and endorse this uniquely written and timely supernatural manual. This literary work is for anyone who desires to see their spiritual eyes opened to learning the various types of angels but importantly how to participate, Word-activate, and operate with the ministry of angels of fire to see signs, miracles, and wonders in your life and to all those around you.

DR. NAIM COLLINS
Prophetic Voice
Author, *Realms of the Prophetic*
Wilmington, Delaware

Candice Smithyman's book *Angels of Fire* is a wonderful book that balances biblical passages on angels with many of her personal experiences with angels. Candice provides many excellent guidelines for interacting with angels every day as well as specific ways we can cooperate with God's fiery messengers to fulfill God's purposes for ourselves and others on the earth. This book is full of wonderful stories about her encounters with angels that can change your life.

JOAN HUNTER
Author/Healing Evangelist

Dr. Candice, you've done it, *Angels of Fire* is a masterpiece! You have managed to uncover the intricacies and complexities of the angelic realm and yet keeping it simple to comprehend and enjoyable for the reader! I love how you've skillfully interwoven personal encounters and stories of angels along with the depth of scripture.

I know I've personally been impacted by angelic encounters since I was 5 years old. I'm so thankful for their involvement and assistance in our everyday life!

Whether you're a new believer or mature leader there's something in this book for you! Read and soar with the Angels into new dimensions of the Lord!

DR. JOSHUA FOWLER
AwakeTheWorld.org
Dallas, Texas
Author of *Pause in My Presence*

ANGELS
OF FIRE

DESTINY IMAGE BOOKS BY CANDICE SMITHYMAN

Releasing Heaven

Releasing Heaven's Atmospheres Into Chaos, Crisis, and Fear

ANGELS OF FIRE

THE MINISTRY OF ANGELS IN END-TIME REVIVAL

CANDICE SMITHYMAN

DESTINY IMAGE® PUBLISHERS, INC.

P.O. Box 310, Shippensburg, PA 17257-0310

"Promoting Inspired Lives."

This book and all other Destiny Image and Destiny Image Fiction books are available at Christian bookstores and distributors worldwide.

Cover design by Eileen Rockwell

For more information on foreign distributors, call 717-532-3040.

Reach us on the Internet: www.destinyimage.com.

ISBN 13 TP: 978-0-7684-5778-0

ISBN 13 eBook: 978-0-7684-5779-7

ISBN 13 HC: 978-0-7684-5781-0

ISBN 13 LP: 978-0-7684-5780-3

For Worldwide Distribution, Printed in the U.S.A.

2 3 4 5 6 7 8 / 25 24 23 22 21

DEDICATION

I would like to dedicate this book to my Lord and Savior, Jesus Christ, who has united me to Father God, and the beautiful sweet presence of the Holy Spirit every day. I also dedicate this book to my amazing husband, Adam Smithyman; my three beautiful children, Alexandria, Nicholas, and Samantha; their spouses, Avery Smithyman and Hunter Lisenba; and my first grandson, Asher Smithyman. And to my mother, Joan Borland Rainsberger, who always encourages me in the supernatural.

ACKNOWLEDGMENTS

I am eternally grateful to my family who sacrificed while I spent the time and effort to bring forth this supernatural message. The one who gets the prize is my husband, Adam Smithyman, for supporting me by always doing duties at home and church which frees me up to write. My daughter Alexandria Knight, who continually edits all my television programs, and my daughter, Samantha, who does the graphics for my social media. My Freedom Destiny Church family and intercessors, and the intercessors for Candice Smithyman Ministries, who helped pray me through this manuscript and press into new territory. The Destiny Image Publishing team of Larry Sparks, Tina Pugh, and Shaun Tabatt who believed in this book before I did. John Martin and Tammy Fitzgerald for editing it so well. For Ryan Bruss who encouraged the original teaching called, "Angels on Assignment" for my *Releasing Heaven* show with Sid Roth. Jackie Duvall, one of the first people to read the book, who gave her suggestions to make it better for all. Sid Roth and his team for encouraging me to teach what God has put on my heart. Connie Janzen, my producer on my ISN *It's Supernatural!* show, *Your Path to Destiny*. My friends and administrative support at Smith Media Group, my *Glory Road* television producer, Dolores Rivera, who has helped *Glory Road* expand into new territories. Laura Douglass from Providence PR, who will get this message into the right hands. My dear friend, Elder Debbi Shon, who stands by me always praying and helping me have the courage to go forward. Pastor Dina Duchene, Dream Mentors Coach Trainer, and Pastor Iana Harris, who pray, uplift, and encourage me and the rest of the elders, staff and church body of Freedom Destiny who I love dearly. Lastly, my sister, Debra Hodgson, who is so precious to me.

CONTENTS

FOREWORD

by Apostle Guillermo Maldonado

THE END-TIME SIGNS ARE GROWING STRONGER AND MORE apparent with each passing day, signaling the approaching second coming of Jesus and the greatest outpouring of His glory. Candice Smithyman's *Angels of Fire* is an important resource to have on hand in preparation for these endtimes. As one of God's appointed prophetic and supernatural ministers, she expertly introduces the topic of angels, God's longtime warriors and helpers, and how they always have been and will be crucial for the coming move of God's glory and how we, as the remnant bride of Jesus, must join them to bring the end-time revival this world needs in anticipation for God's return. Informative as it is powerful, this book will equip you for the end-time revival that is soon to come. Let us welcome Jesus alert and ready, for He is coming back for a vigilant bride. Maranatha, He is coming soon!

—APOSTLE GUILLERMO MALDONADO
Senior Pastor of King Jesus Ministry
Author of *Jesus Is Coming Soon, Created for Purpose, How to Walk in the Supernatural Power of God,* and others

PREAMBLE

I AM SO BLESSED YOU DECIDED TO READ *Angels of Fire: The Ministry of Angels in End-Time Revival.* This book is a supernatural manual on how to participate with the angelic hosts to see signs, miracles, and wonders happen around you as you participate with God for kingdom revival. I am writing this book today because of a series of supernatural encounters that prompted its release.

On July 19, 2020, I was driving in my car to Tampa, Florida. I was to be a guest on *The Good Life* with Bob and Jane D'Andrea, the founders of Christian Television Network. The Lord spoke to me about two books that He wanted me to write. One of those was a book on fire angels and my experiences with and insights into angels. When I completed my drive, I recorded in my notes on my phone my encounter with Lord and the books He wanted me to write. A week later, I got an email from my publisher, Destiny Image, asking me to write a book on fire angels and angels in the end-time revival. I was so surprised! I was under contract to write a different book for Destiny Image, so I asked them about that one and they said, "We believe God wants this one released in advance." Apparently, they felt the Lord leading them that very week at a meeting they had at Sid Roth's *It's Supernatural!* studios, where I had done a master class on angels that was released on Sid Roth's *It's Supernatural!* show. Apparently, after my guest appearance surrounding my book *Releasing Heaven: Creating a Supernatural Environment through Heavenly Encounters* and the angel master class that was offered with the book, they felt it engaging enough to audiences that they wanted to offer more teaching on angelic activity, participating with the angels of fire, and how all of this will impact the end-time church and revival in our world.

I was excited but, of course, apprehensive as I did not want this book to be only a theological discourse on angels. There are many books out there on that subject. I wanted this book to be experiential and one that would draw people into a deeper relationship with God and an understanding of how to cooperate with Holy Spirit and angels in the supernatural. When we open our eyes today, we see a difficult world that needs the kingdom of God made manifest. Angels will help usher in the great awakening and revival in our nations. They are simply creatures God created, and when we know how they operate, we can have faith to join God and them in the next great global glory on earth.

As you read the pages of this book, just know God wanted a supernatural manual to the angelic that would increase the faith of His people to step out and begin engaging with the angelic hosts, who will usher in the revival in the endtimes. God wants us in cooperation with Him for end-time revival, and that means we must learn to be in cooperation with the heavenly hosts. However, many of us don't even know or understand we have angels assigned to us or what they even do in and around us. This book is a way to begin to open your eyes to this type of relationship with God in the supernatural and to His supernatural beings who respond to His voice daily.

God has given you His voice in His Word and He wants you to begin to use it and have your eyes opened to the fact that the angels will join in the word you speak on God's behalf. You have legions of angels surrounding you as God uses you to press into darkness and be the light. As we the church of Jesus Christ learn to live in the victory we have in Jesus' death, burial, resurrection, and ascension, we receive a critical opportunity to participate more with angels and learn to be agents of rulership in the earth during the endtimes. This book will also give you scientific insight into the colors of fire angels, healing of angels and disorders, hierarchy of angels, the throne room of God, and characteristics of God. I believe your eyes will be opened in such a way that you will fall more in love with Jesus as you learn about Him and who He is in the throne room with His angels. I have done a lot of research in this book that shows how the earth realm is a manifestation of heaven. Please join me on a journey of faith as we examine how to live our lives amongst the angelic and the supernatural encounters of God as we wait eagerly for revival awakening.

INTRODUCTION

WELCOME TO *Angels of Fire: The Ministry of Angels in the End-Time Revival*, where you will learn about the different angels that God has created and how to participate with them in His kingdom plan and purpose. God wants you to be a part of kingdom rulership, but you must learn to participate with the angelic host to bring this forth. In this book, you are going to learn how angels are on assignment to help us fulfill the call of God on our lives. Angels are always working around us. In order to participate with angels, we must cultivate a mind-set for the angelic. We must understand the victory the church of Jesus Christ has been given through the death, burial, and resurrection of Jesus and His ascension. There is power in the ascension. The church and the heavenly hosts work together in unity to bring kingdom rulership to the earth.

As we begin this book, I want to pray that your spiritual senses will be opened so you can open your mind to principles of the resurrection, ascension, victory, and overcoming power that we have to rule earth and how to recognize angelic activity that will bring heaven to earth. I also want your heart opened to receive supernatural insight on angels and how God has created them to be a part of His universe to serve His kingdom purposes. You are a part of that kingdom purpose, and God wants you to know how to work with angels so He can advance His mission on the earth. When the angelic host and humanity come together for God, we can overthrow the strongholds of the enemy and see deliverance and healing. We can be change agents for God to release the glory in and through us. God wants to use you and the angelic host working together.

Lord, I pray today that my friends' eyes are opened to the supernatural and they can begin to access the supernatural by faith, knowing that You created angels to bring about Your kingdom plan and You had an intent that they would work together with the human race to bring about change in the earth today. Thank You, Jesus, for opening up the portals of heaven and bringing forth revelation knowledge concerning all types of angels and how to work with them.

Please keep an open heart in the spirit realms to the words on these pages. This book is not a textbook on the heavenly hosts; it is not a theological discourse on the angelic, though theologically it is sound; it is not a medical book. This book is a supernatural tool to help you grow in the knowledge of God, yourself, and the angelic hosts and how all three aspects of the universe come together to work for the good of the kingdom. Throughout the book, keep your heart and mind open to the knowledge of God, the supernatural, the prophetic, the power of the Holy Spirit, and your role in presenting the kingdom of God on earth.

When you view things from this perspective, you will enjoy this book as a manual of supernatural insight into spiritual things. I believe God is going to take you on a beautiful journey of faith, knowing more of Him and the role of angels in your life and the kingdom. Grow deeper in your love for God and your faith will be increased and you will understand how to participate with the angelic and move mountains in the supernatural.

PRAYER OF IMPARTATION

I want to pray for you today so that you can grab hold of the fact that God has assigned an angel to you, even many angels, and He wants you to be able to activate those angels, participate with those angels, and be a part of what God is doing in and around you. You are also a member of Christ's very own body, and He wants you to know your life is hidden with Him so you can walk in the fullness of God on the earth today. You are a member of Christ's body that has ascended and is seated with Him. This power alone will change how you navigate the earth realm and sense and work alongside angels for end-time revival.

> *Father, we just thank You so much for Your presence, Your overwhelming presence, Father, and the fact that You've assigned an angel to us, Lord, and that angels are there to watch over us. I just ask that each person who reads today will have an angel activation, that their eyes will be open, that they will see into the spirit realms, that they will truly be able to grab hold of what You're doing. We just pray for an activation of that seer anointing to come upon each and every person, and that by the*

end of this book they would have read so much on angels and their assignments in our lives that they would better understand their position and power as kingdom rulers. They would learn to live out the principles of resurrection and ascension as we cohabitate with heaven and see end-time revival and awakening in our universe. I pray they would be able to step out in the faith of God and see angels in operation around them.

Even now you are beginning to have your faith increased. Please continue to pray this prayer each time you read each chapter so that you will be able to quicken your spirit and soul to the new revelation knowledge God wants to bring you concerning the victory of His church and His angelic hosts in the endtimes.

Fire Angels Dispatched

Testimony of Healing from COVID-19

It started on a Thursday, beginning with a cough. I tested positive on Sunday. The first week it got a little worse each day, but overall I thought I had a mild case.

I got sicker and weaker for 17 days straight. I lost 17 pounds in 17 days. Close friends and ministry connections quickly went to their knees for me. My Tuesday night prayer group called me and prayed as a group for me on the phone, claiming the blood of Jesus and encouraging me to have faith instead of fear. They sang and praised God for my future healing and were a great encouragement. I cried and listened and quietly thanked them after about an hour.

I couldn't talk without coughing. I couldn't complete a sentence without losing my breath. I communicated my needs to my sweet wife in short phrases and one-word requests. Discouraging, to say the least.

Mostly, I talked to God. I prayed constantly.

"Lord," I said, *"if it's time for me to come home, I'm ready. If this is the end of my spiritual warfare ministry for You, I'm good with that. I'm tired. I am hurting. I confess my fear of not being able to breathe."*

I began to realize this might be the end of earthly me. I started to picture seeing my dad again, grandparents who have gone ahead, and loved ones I miss who had finished their walk. It was actually both exciting and scary.

But as I sat and thought through all this, it felt wrong. It felt as if I still had work to do, ministry to do, encouragement to hand out, and God's love to share with hurting people. I was very conflicted, though I didn't share these intimate thoughts with anyone.

My negative side realized there were many details of daily life that my wife (a schoolteacher) would struggle to figure out if I went on to heaven. I needed to fix this before the end, if this was the end.

"Babe," I began, "the truth is I am not getting better, and I need you to video me showing you how to do some things." She didn't argue. It's only a backup plan, right?

So we would record one thing, and I would rest and take some more pills. We would record something else, and I would try to eat or take a nap. This went on for a couple of days. We covered how to order my books from Amazon at the author's price, how to do the online banking, and how the bills were reconciled and paid.

She never complained. She never cried (in front of me at least). She also never told me to stop. We both knew we were staring a crisis in the face, and it could go either way (which was later confirmed by my doctor).

At one point we went to the ER for evaluation. I was getting worse, and everyone really knew it. After the evaluation, the ER doctor met with us.

"What do you recommend?" we asked.

"I'd really like to put you in the hospital," he replied, "so we can keep you here and see when a bed becomes available." We were at their separate ER facility, and there were no beds available in the hospital. Wow.

We asked if there were any other options and discovered we could go home, taking oxygen with us, so that's what we did. This was five days in.

About ten days in, I couldn't eat. So here I am on an insulin pump, sugars running a little high, and no appetite. For the first time in 45 years as a diabetic, I went a full day with almost nothing to eat; I just couldn't get it down.

It was at about this time that I began to learn the "sacrifice of praise." I would pray and thank God and praise Him in spite of my circumstances. I would raise my hands and thank Him. I thanked Him for all He had already done, for the privilege of suffering for the kingdom, and for being at home during my final days instead of in the hospital, isolated and alone. I cried and praised, truly a sacrifice in the face of my ongoing struggle. It felt good.

That day (day 16) I finished one of my critical medications, and the next day, the Lord's Day, I was able to eat a little. It wasn't much, but it was better than nothing, and I knew I absolutely had to eat, or I would be on a ventilator soon.

Although I began to eat a little better, it was obvious I wasn't improving. I was just holding my own—barely.

By Saturday, day 17, I was at a critical point. We had just added a new antibiotic and scheduled another TeleMed session with the doctor for Monday. We were desperately praying for the new medicine and for God to come through with a miracle.

That's when I decided to make a public request on my Facebook page for prayer. At this point I wanted all the prayers I could get, and I still felt God had more work for me to do here and now. Here is what I posted at 9:45 a.m.:

"Prayer request: I've been diabetic for 45 years. I am very sick with COVID. It's day 17 and I've been getting weaker every day. Please post a prayer for me if you feel called to. Or fast for me. Thank you."

It got 642 likes, 832 comments, and 129 shares that went all over the world. Only God can do that.

At 1:58 p.m. that afternoon, I got a text from my friend, Candice Smithyman:

"Hi Steve! How are you doing? Emily Rose told me you were recovering from COVID. Praying healing for you in Jesus' name! Candice."

I replied with, "The problem is I'm not recovering. Thank you for the prayers."

She replied with, "I was speaking in faith! You are recovering in Jesus' name! I believe this!"

"Amen. I stand in agreement."

Then the most exciting reply arrived: "I asked the Lord to dispatch the blue seraphim angels that bring copper sulfate to your body for strength to your bones so they glow and you begin to be revived in your bones! Blue fire angels kill properties that hurt our immune system. The orange fire angels carry calcium sulfate from throne of God also and break immune disorders! We pray this for you and your family! May joy increase by Holy Spirit as a merry heart does the body good! You are getting healthy and God is surrounding you with these fire angels to purify your lungs and immune system! In Jesus' name! Begin to laugh no matter how you feel and this will break off!"

Wow. "I'm already laughing in celebration," I responded.

"Amen! A merry heart does the bones good and when your bones glow everything on the bones must explode with life-giving properties from your cells! Proverbs 17:22, 'A merry heart does good, like medicine, but a broken spirit dries the bones.' Proverbs 3:8 MSG, 'Your body will glow with health, your very bones will vibrate with life!' ...Keep me posted!"

I said, "Amen."

As I leaned back in my recliner and began to doze off, I noticed a warmth in my feet, and I began to feel like I was floating on air, smooth and very comfortable. It started on the bottom of my feet and traveled up my body. I felt the warm feeling of pure peace. Then I went on to sleep. I woke up at 3 a.m. feeling *good* for the first time in 18 days! Then I woke again at 6 a.m. feeling good and hungry. Later I remembered how many times Jesus would raise someone from the dead and then instruct those around to give them something to eat:

*And at that moment **her life returned**, and she immediately stood up! Then **Jesus told them to give her something to eat*** (Luke 8:55 NLT).

Prior to this I had just been making myself eat because I had no appetite at all. My wife cooked me what tasted like the best eggs and sausage I have ever had!

Steve Hemphill
Author/Speaker/Teacher
My Search for the Real Heaven
My Search for Prayers Satan Hates
What Are the Stakes?
God's Power for Our Daily Battles
Active-Faith.org

CHAPTER 1

FAITH FOR THE ANGELIC

*In speaking of the angels he says, "He makes his
angels spirits, and his servants flames of fire."*
—HEBREWS 1:7
The voice of the Lord divideth the flames of fire.
—PSALM 29:7 KJV
For our God is a consuming fire.
—HEBREWS 12:29 KJV

FIRE IS A KEY ASPECT OF WHO GOD IS. HIS ANGELS ARE A PIECE of Him and are servants that carry His characteristics to the earth. If God is a God of fire, all-consuming fire, and He is One who purifies us and sanctifies us, then the angels are going to have a piece of His fire to bring to us. When God dispatches them on our behalf, they will carry a characteristic of Him, just like a servant carries a characteristic of a master, just like a student carries a characteristic of a teacher, and just like a child carries a characteristic of a parent. The angels are characteristic of who He is. When they come and are dispatched on our behalf because of His command and because of us holding firm to the Word of God, then they carry His authority to perform His Word as an extension of Him.

When we talk about fire angels, this is not something crazy or weird, as an angel is in the presence of God and carries the characteristics of God to the earth. God is love, so there are angels that will, when they're around us, cause us to feel overwhelming love. There are angels that are characteristic of God's desire to replenish or bring resources. They will bring a part of God to the earth in that area and replenish us. They will restore us. God is a healer, and fire angels come and carry healing to the earth. The Holy Spirit does all of those things, but angels are a kind of species external to Him that extend His traits. Angels don't need salvation. Therefore, they are part of the characteristics of Father, Son, and Holy Spirit.

When you look at angels, imagine them as being these guards who carry all of the characteristics of the Father, Son, and Holy Spirit. It's alright to be connected with them because they are created, just like we are created. They're created for unique purposes for heaven and earth.

The amazing thing is that we as humans are created in the image of God. Genesis 1:27 says, "So God created mankind in his own image, in the image of God he created them; male and female he created them." Angels have properties like God and His throne, but we are created beings in the very image of God. God has special purposes for us in His kingdom and for them. We must all learn to work together, especially now in the endtimes. This is why this revelation of angels of fire is important to grab hold of. One of our purposes is to become glory portals ourselves to activate the kingdom of heaven on earth.

I want you to really grab hold of the purpose of angels. They're messengers, they're waiters, they do His bidding, and they carry His glory because they are bringing a part of God to us. Our salvation, healing, restoration, and all of the amazing things that happen to us are a part of Father, Son, and Holy Spirit, and angels are extensions of the Father. We just learn to participate with them. I'm asking God to remove a veil from your eyes. Just as you see a human person sitting next to you, may the veil be removed in the name of Jesus, so now you can see an angel sitting next to you. They are right next to you. They are just in a different realm from you, whereas the Holy Spirit is on the inside of you, if you are a believer. He's right with you because of what Jesus did. But the angel is sitting next to you. We are all a part of the army of God in the endtimes.

I hope this gives you a clearer picture of what the supernatural realm looks like. So when you're around the table with your friends or your family, Mom and Dad sitting in their seats and the kids, if we pull back the veil, all of their angels are sitting there too. So I pray that the veil is removed from your eyes, and you see into the supernatural realms.

In Psalm 91:9-16 we read:

> *If you say, "The Lord is my refuge," and you make the Most High your dwelling, no harm will overtake you, no disaster will come near your tent. For he will command his angels concerning you to guard you in all your ways; they will lift you up in their hands, so that you will not strike your foot against a stone. You will tread on the*

lion and the cobra; you will trample the great lion and the serpent. "Because he loves me," says the Lord, "I will rescue him; I will protect him, for he acknowledges my name. He will call on me, and I will answer him; I will be with him in trouble, I will deliver him and honor him. With long life I will satisfy him and show him my salvation."

The angels are a part of God's protection plan for us. He assigns them as we call on Him and rest in Him and His provision. Your guardian angel has a purpose, the hierarchy of angels has a purpose, and we as humans have a purpose, and we are all united together by our creator Himself, God.

FAITH TO SEE

If you want to learn to engage with the angels, then you must first learn to live by faith. The realms of faith are needed in order to understand the supernatural and how it works in our world today. Faith comes by hearing and hearing by the Word of God (see Rom. 10:17). We must know and understand what the scriptures say about faith. In Hebrews 11:6, the Word reads:

And without faith it is impossible to please God, because anyone who comes to him must believe that he exists and that he rewards those who earnestly seek him.

If we want to please God, the only way to do this is to live a life of faith. Faith is not seeing in the natural; it is seeing in the spiritual first and then calling it forth in the natural.

In Hebrews 11:1, the Word says, "Now faith is the substance of things hoped for, the evidence of things not seen" (KJV). This scripture defines faith a substance or a reality. Faith is a tangible reality of what we believe. Faith is something we can sink our teeth into. It is something that we can touch through our spiritual senses in such a way that it appears to have a natural component to it. That is the kind of faith needed for the endtimes—faith that pleases God and sets us up for rulership in the kingdom. This kind of God-faith will open up doors of reality for you to begin to participate with the heavenly host to see God's purposes come to pass on the earth now and during the end-time revival.

The apostle Paul speaks about the God-kind of faith we are to have if we want to engage with the supernatural. Galatians 2:20 reads, "I am crucified with Christ: nevertheless I live; yet not I, but Christ liveth in me: and the life which I now live in the flesh I live by the faith of the Son of God, who loved me, and gave himself for me" (KJV).

The faith of God is having the kind of faith that God has for a situation. It is not an earthly type of faith. It is a type of faith where we know that God said it and we can see, hear, smell, taste, and touch with our five spiritual senses the same atmosphere of reality that God has. It is knowing that God will indeed do something; that is His will based on His nature. God is love, peace, justice, mercy, kindness, joy, healing, provision, righteousness, and so on. He has many attributes, and the faith of God is backed by these very attributes of God. When we have the faith of God, we are saying that we have backed our thoughts on who He is in every respect. That if He said it, it will be done! That if He willed it, it will come to pass. That we can bank on what He said and His desire to see who He is in the world come to pass through His hands and feet, who are us, and His angelic hosts who work for

Him also. If we want to experience angels, we must have the faith of God that angels exist and we must know that God created them for a purpose.

We build this faith by knowing God and by knowing His Word. As you read this book, I pray you will learn more about God's love for you and how He has designed the universe for you to engage with Him and with His angelic hosts. God wants what is best for us all, but we must be thinking like Him. He is around angels all day. They are at His throne night and day. They sing and worship and do His bidding night and day. We must believe what the Word says about what these assigned creatures do so that we can indeed have the faith of God concerning them. God does not doubt He has angels or even doubt they will do what He says. He knows they will follow and obey; they see themselves as creatures that are called to do His bidding and perform His Word. He knows this, and we should too. When we adopt how God feels about His own angels, we will open up a portal by faith where the angels will come to minister to us and with us for God and His kingdom purpose.

PRAYER OF FAITH

You are only one step away from walking in this truth daily. If you want the faith of God, ask God now. Pray:

> *Lord Jesus, please give me Your faith so that I can believe in angels and that You love me and have assigned one to me and that, as a citizen of heaven first, You have asked me to participate with angels for Your kingdom purpose.*

The Word says we are citizens of heaven in Philippians 3:19-21, which reads:

> *Their mind is set on earthly things. But our citizenship is in heaven. And we eagerly await a Savior from there, the Lord Jesus Christ, who, by the power that enables him to bring everything under his control, will transform our lowly bodies so that they will be like his glorious body.*

If we have faith that angels are in existence, we can have a faith that will help the manifestation of those angels happen around us. We may not see them with natural eyes, but we can feel them and sense them with our five spiritual senses of sight, hearing, smell, taste, and touch. Mature Christians learn to discern the spiritual things this way. I pray you learn this in this book. James 2:18-19 reads:

> *But someone will say, "You have faith; I have deeds." Show me your faith without deeds, and I will show you my faith by my deeds.*

I am speaking of having faith with deeds. If you believe the Word and that angels are there to perform the Word, then you will believe when you speak the Word that they will be there. Your faith will have a deed outcome. You will see the manifestation of your spiritual faith of God in the natural. We must have faith to see the angelic realm.

CHILDLIKE FAITH

God not only calls our faith to be like His, but also to be childlike faith. Children see angels much more than adults. When my daughter Alexandria was small, she would tell us that angels were in her room. I could not see them, but she would tell me they were there. I believed her, but I would look at the space she saw and think, "I don't see anything she sees, but they must be there; I just don't have enough childlike faith." I believe babies can see angels in action very easily. Have you ever watched a baby's eyes light up when they are not even looking at you? What are they looking at? Sure, it can be nerve impulses in their brain, but seriously what do we really know about any of this? We must have childlike faith. What you believe will manifest. Do you have childlike faith? The angelic realm is real, but it manifests by faith. Matthew 18:1-4 reads:

> At that time the disciples came to Jesus and asked, "Who, then, is the greatest in the kingdom of heaven?" He called a little child to him, and placed the child among them. And he said: "Truly I tell you, unless you change and become like little children, you will never enter the kingdom of heaven. Therefore, whoever takes the lowly position of this child is the greatest in the kingdom of heaven.

God expects us to have childlike faith so we can live out the kingdom of heaven on earth. Angels are a manifestation of the kingdom of heaven on earth. If we want to participate with angels, we must have faith like a child.

You are stepping into that place of believing for revelation and understanding about your angels and how you can participate with them. I believe, in Jesus' name, the Spirit of the Lord is lifting your faith and will give you some supernatural encounters with angels that will forever change your life. You must begin to know and understand where angels inhabit. They live where the Word is, where light is, where the temple is, where purity is. These are the habitations or culture of angelic activity. You will see and experience angelic activity if you open yourself to recognizing what is in your environment that is holy, righteous, and like Jesus.

If we are going to activate the angels in our lives, it is through the Word of God and experience of Holy Spirit that we grow in understanding of angels and the supernatural. We cannot be passive in our belief but active. Faith is a substance or a reality, and when we believe in something we move in it. We must really get involved with the Word of God, who is Jesus—not just actively hearing the Word, which increases our faith, but really making the Word a part of who we are through actions (deeds) that come by faith. The more you read the Word, the more you're going to be able to see into the spirit realms. God will begin to make His Word come alive.

MIND-SETS FOR THE ANGELIC

Everyone wants to see the angelic, but you have to harbor a mind-set that will open up heavenly habitations for the angelic to come forth. One of the ways to do this is to create a mind-set for angelic activity and cognitive awareness by faith that angels are present. Whether you see them or not in the natural, they are present and they are activated by faith and the Word. There are also specific atmospheres that will foster angelic activity, which we will discuss further. We can be co-creators with God in the earth realm by faith and simply create habitations for angels and they will come automatically. Light and fire are attributes of God, and when these commodities are present the heavenlies will draw manifestations of angelic activity. The glory light of God is a normal presence for angels. Therefore, when they are around light and fire here on earth, they come to rest.

If things are dark, sick, and poverty-stricken, God can change an atmosphere by sending an angel to represent Himself in a lack place, dark place, or place of poverty and lies, and this will open up a portal for the truth and a manifestation from heaven. Because angels are heavenly first, when they show up, heaven shows up. When heaven shows up, atmospheres shift. If God wants to change an earthly scene, He sends a supernatural being from heaven or a supernatural manifestation from heaven to make it happen. These supernatural beings are commanded by Him; they carry His authority, so their atmospheres shift as a result.

When God wanted to shift the atmosphere of the upper room, what did He do? He sent tongues of fire. These tongues of fire were carried from His altar to the people. The fire angels were a part of carrying forth the purified fire to the lips of those who waited in the upper room. I will share more about the purified fire of angels in later chapters, but you can see God changed the earthly atmosphere with a heavenly fire touch. In Acts 2:1-4 the scripture reads:

> And when the day of Pentecost was fully come, they were all with one accord in one place. And suddenly there came a sound from heaven as of a rushing mighty wind, and it filled all the house where they were sitting. And there appeared unto them cloven tongues like as of fire, and it sat upon each of them. And they were all filled with the Holy Ghost, and began to speak with other tongues, as the Spirit gave them utterance (KJV).

Then the whole atmosphere changed because God showed up, and it says Peter stood up and said:

> *But Peter, standing up with the eleven, lifted up his voice, and said unto them, Ye men of Judaea, and all ye that dwell at Jerusalem, be this known unto you, and hearken to my words: for these are not drunken, as ye suppose, seeing it is but the third hour of the day. But this is that which was spoken by the prophet Joel; and it shall come to pass in the last days, saith God, I will pour out of my Spirit upon all flesh: and your sons and your daughters shall prophesy, and your young men shall see visions, and your old men shall dream dreams: and on my servants and on my handmaidens I will pour out in those days of my Spirit; and they shall prophesy: and I will shew wonders in heaven above, and signs in the earth beneath; blood, and fire, and vapour of smoke: the sun shall be turned into darkness, and the moon into blood, before the great and notable day of the Lord come: and it shall come to pass, that whosoever shall call on the name of the Lord shall be saved* (Acts 2:14-21 KJV).

In this passage, the atmosphere was so changed by God that people now felt drunk in the Spirit, and this was in accordance with the prophetic word from Joel in Joel 2:28-32. This prophetic word was now taking place in the church in Acts 2. The angels were present during this. You may say, "Dr. Candice, it does not say that in scripture." It doesn't have to because you know it to be true when you understand the heavenly habitations that angels gravitate toward. Keep your mind open in faith, as I have much to teach you in later chapters concerning purification by fire and how the angels are present when this happens.

Heavenly habitations are where heaven comes and resides in the earth realm. When we remain seated with Christ in heavenly places in our spirit and soul as the apostle Paul tells us in Ephesians 2:6, then we are living in heavenly places and can then dictate change on the earth. Through Jesus' death, burial, and resurrection, we have overcome sin, death, and the grave, and through Christ's ascension we, the church body of believers, are now placed in a position where we are seated with Christ in heavenly places according to the Word of God. We're seated at the right hand of the Father, right where Jesus says He ascended and took the church with Him, so that's where we are today in spirit. When our mental focus is from that position, then we are doing everything in the earth realm from that position. Our spirit is seated with Christ in heavenly places, and if we want to see a habitation for angels, we need to make our earthly environments like that of heaven.

We need to begin to think, to feel, to respond like heaven, and then the angels are going to come and congregate. The angels come where certain atmospheres are. Yes, it's true that God will bring angels to invade an environment that is ungodly or does not even have a habitation of heaven and that He will call them to make a change in that environment. We can invite heaven to be a part of an earthly environment or an environment that is negative or demonic, but it is also true that if we create heavenly habitations we're going to find that the angels are going to come and want to be with us and congregate with us. For instance, if we are gathering together in an environment where there is worship, where there is praise to the Lord, where there is a celebration of communion and the people of the Lord coming together in the earth to praise His name, the angels will come and they will join with us. They will come and join in with the environment that we're creating in the earth, which is like a heavenly environment. When we come to praise and when we come to worship, we're inviting heaven to come to earth, so the angels will naturally congregate there.

One such environment where this is evident is in the throne room of God. There is worship there continually. This atmosphere of praise and adoration is where God resides and His cherubim are with Him in this place.

> *And the four beasts had each of them six wings about him;*
> *and they were full of eyes within: and they rest not day*
> *and night, saying, Holy, holy, holy, Lord God Almighty,*
> *which was, and is, and is to come* (Revelation 4:8 KJV).

This atmosphere is the atmosphere of the throne in heaven. We can simulate this here on earth, and the angels will come congregate with us.

YOU CAN CHANGE ATMOSPHERES

When there's no sign at all of heaven being around and we enter into those environments, as long as we know who we are in Christ and we respond as the victorious church of Jesus Christ, who has ascended with Christ in heavenly places, then we can change our environment and the angels will come and join us in that place. They will be kingdom co-workers with us. They will be participators. They will be the waiters that come and join us in the work that we are doing. Now, let me just share with you from scripture some examples of specific environmental differences and how a habitation or portal to heaven was created by an angel sent at God's command and then the atmosphere shifted for God's purpose.

Let's reference the story of Joseph and Mary. Joseph had planned to wed Mary but found out she was pregnant and then wanted to divorce her. Joseph felt betrayed by Mary; she was not unfaithful, as she was found to be pregnant by the Holy Spirit, but Joseph could not comprehend this scenario in the natural. He had plans to break off the engagement. He was going to do what every person does—take matters into his own hands. But God gave him a dream. We read in Matthew 1:18-25:

> *This is how the birth of Jesus the Messiah came about: His mother Mary was pledged to be married to Joseph, but before they came together, she was found to be pregnant through the Holy Spirit. Because Joseph her husband was faithful to the law, and yet did not want to expose her to public disgrace, he had in mind to divorce her quietly. But after he had considered this, an angel of the Lord appeared to him in a dream and said, "Joseph son of David, do not be afraid to take Mary home as your wife, because what is conceived in her is from the Holy Spirit. She will give birth to a son, and you are to give him the name Jesus, because he will save his people from their sins." All this took place to fulfill what the Lord had said through the prophet: "The virgin will conceive and give birth to a son, and they will call him Immanuel" (which means "God with us"). When Joseph woke up, he did what the angel of the Lord had commanded him and took Mary home as his wife. But he did not consummate*

their marriage until she gave birth to a son. And he gave him the name Jesus.

ANGELS CAN CHANGE LACK TO FULLNESS

When the angel came and spoke to Joseph in the dream, it was because Joseph was in a state of lack—a deficit. In other words, Joseph was in need of heaven to come and reach out to him or else he was going to end up divorcing Mary. And so we see that many times angels are sent to us from heaven in order to awaken us to our lack thinking or fear with a message from heaven to keep us inside the sovereign will of God. Joseph was in a place of fear and lack, and God sent an angel to him in a dream to speak to him, "Joseph, son of David, do not be afraid to take Mary home as your wife, because what is conceived in her is from the Holy Spirit." The angel then gave a prophecy of how the earth would be changed— Mary would give birth to a son, and they were to give him the name Jesus, because He would save His people from their sins.

I find it very interesting that Joseph was living in a state of lack and fear when he was about to become the earthly father of the Savior. Jesus would save him from his very fear and lack. God will often send angels to change an environment from fear and anxiety. God will send angels in order to say, "Heaven's here," and God is with you in the midst of what you're going through. When Jesus was tempted by the devil in the wilderness after 40 days of fasting in Matthew 4:11, we find that the enemy knew the power that Jesus had as the Son of God and heir to the throne. The enemy spoke to Jesus: "I already know who You are and that You are the Son of God and You're in the fullness of God." Now, one of the aspects of the Son of God who reigns in heaven, who lives in a heavenly habitation, is that He is surrounded by angels. The devil actually knew this fact. So he challenged Jesus during His weak moment by saying:

> And saith unto him, If thou be the Son of God, cast thyself down: for it is written, He shall give his angels charge concerning thee: and in their hands they shall bear thee up, lest at any time thou dash thy foot against a stone (Matthew 4:6 KJV).

Jesus didn't accept that offer. Instead, He answered with scripture, saying, "It is written again, Thou shalt not tempt the Lord thy God" (Matt. 4:7 KJV). The fullness of God will attract the angels of God. The fullness of God is witnessed on the throne of God and everywhere God is, so angels will migrate to this level of fullness. We can create this fullness in the earth realm by living in the reality of the heavenly realms by faith. Remember, faith is the reality of things we hope for (see Heb. 11:1), so as you hope for heavenly habitations and live as though they are a reality, you will create this kind of environment for heaven to come to earth.

PRAYER FOR CHANGING ATMOSPHERES

Lord Jesus, help me to have the faith of God to be an agent used of You to change my environments. When I worship You, the angels surround me and come into the environments that I am in. I am a glory portal or carrier of Your glory and so the angels are all around me. Help me to go into difficult environments like my home life or my workplace or my neighborhood and bring with me the glory of heaven so that the angels will be following me into the places You want to impact for the kingdom. Thank You for using me in this way. Help me to know that as angels surrounded Jesus they surround me, not because of my good works but because of what Jesus did for me. This makes me an heir of the King and one who carries the signet ring of the King. Therefore, I can change environments and angels will then come inhabit there.

CHAPTER 2

HEAVENLY HABITATIONS

A s you learned in the last chapter, you can bring heaven to earth and the angels will come and join you. There are earth realms and heavenly realms that we can choose by faith to live in. Realms are dimensions that we access by faith in who we are in Christ and what He has done for us through our death, burial, resurrection, and ascension in Him. Once we understand angels and their work in the earth and our participation with them, we cannot go further in our study until we understand how they migrate to places that are like their heavenly habitations. Yes, we can create heavenly habitations in the earth realm we live in by faith. These heavenly habitations are intensified when we understand the power of ascension. What is the power of ascension? It is understanding that by faith we can create an atmosphere on the earth that is heavenly because we live by faith in Ephesians 2:6 that we're seated with Christ in heavenly places. This kind of ascension atmosphere invites the angels to come and make a habitation in the earth realm.

END-TIME REVIVAL MIND-SET

People who have an ascension mind-set live in the fullness of their spirit and soul as a heavenly habitation. Because of that, the angels are present around them to protect them. Why? Because God assigns them to care for us, those whom He loves. We know that Jesus had angels around Him all the time and at any moment He could call on them. We create heavenly habitations if we have the mind-set of heaven, knowing we are seated with Christ in heavenly places. Then we will begin to act and respond in faith that way. Then the angels will come around that environment.

Now, when we talk about the end-time revival, we must know that we are the church that has ascended. Jesus died, was buried, and was resurrected. He got the keys to Hades and the grave, and sin and death were defeated. After this, He resurrected and later He ascended. When He ascended, He brought us with Him, and so we are there with Him in that heavenly place in the spirit even though our bodies are here in the earth realm. When we operate in the earth realm with our spirit and our soul, from our seat with Christ in heavenly places we can activate ascension atmospheres. Although your body is here in the earth, your thoughts in your mind, your emotional state in your soul, and your spirit man are connected to that heavenly place when you live the ascended life on the earth.

When we live like this, we the church are being the end-time church. We are being the New Testament church. We are being the church that God wants us to be. When we are the church that way, then we have the confidence that the angels are partnering with us. The angels are living today even in this moment from an end-time atmosphere perspective. We need to understand our power and ability to release heaven's power in the earth, along with commanding the angels by speaking the Word of God. We do not pray to angels; we speak God's Word and the angels respond.

ANGELS NEED NO SALVATION

Hebrews 1:14 says, "Are not all angels ministering spirits sent to serve those who will inherit salvation?" We are an entirely different species from the angels, but we cohabitate with the angels and they are responsive to us. We are heirs of salvation. They are not—they did not need to be saved. There was no sin in them. They live in the heavenly and earth realms without sin being an issue for them.

They are in existence to fulfill kingdom purpose and support the heirs of God. This is important information when we ponder the church in the endtimes and prepare for revival in the nations. Where should the soul of the church be? What mind-set should the church have? How can the church access its heavenly resources bought with the precious blood of Jesus? Good questions—please keep reading for more revelation.

PREPARATION FOR REVIVAL IN THE ENDTIMES

We need to know that an end-time church is a church that understands an ascension perspective. The end-time church is a church that knows collectively that it's seated in heavenly places with Christ and is continuously victorious. As we view our world from the perspective of ruling and reigning with Christ when He returns to the earth, we must change our perspective of who we are in Him. His seat of authority is in heaven and He gave us this same authority. The head of the church, Jesus Christ, has control and we, His body, flow with Him. The church is to respond like Him in the earth because they know that they are indeed, in spirit, already seated with Christ in heavenly places. Therefore, the end-time church's operation in the earth realm is from that mind-set.

When we have that level of mind-set, we are positioning ourselves to partner with the angels for end-time revival. Revival is when the church itself knows that it's ascended. We are not just the resurrected church. Yes, the church resurrected and sin, death, and the grave have been overcome, but the church has ascended. The church's position on the earth now is like we are back in the Garden of Eden before Adam and Eve's sin caused separation from God. When Adam and Eve ate the forbidden fruit, they took us to the place of toil, of having a curse upon us. They took us to that place of fear, a place where we were separated from God and therefore death entered. But when Jesus resurrected and got the keys of Hades, He removed the stronghold of satan. Now we are ascended because He ascended and we, His body, are with our Head, Jesus.

Jesus showed Himself to His disciples for a certain period of time after the resurrection, and then He ascended. When He ascended, He took His seat next to the Father. That's where the church, who is in Him, is seated now. When the apostle Paul spoke to the church at Colossae, he said this:

> *If ye then be risen with Christ, seek those things which are above, where Christ sitteth on the right hand of God. Set your affection on things above, not on things on the earth.*

For ye are dead, and your life is hid with Christ in God. When Christ, who is our life, shall appear, then shall ye also appear with him in glory (Colossians 3:1-4 KJV).

The church's life is hidden with Christ in God, and our thoughts are to be with Christ seated in these places. Because of Jesus' death, burial, resurrection, and ascension to the heavenly seat, we, the end-time church, now have a new relationship with the Father. We are in the Son of God, no longer separated from the Father. We are that close to God every day, but we have to live from that heavenly place in spirit, soul, and body on the earth. While we're on the earth, that place is a place of fullness in our spirit and soul. It is not a place of lack, poverty, deficit, or fear. It is not a place of separation. We can be full here in our earthly existence.

This fullness is where the angels reside. So if you want to see angels manifest in the earth, then you need to position yourself with that kind of mind-set. Then angels will join you in your work. Angels come where there's faith. Faith tells us that we are in the ascension place with Jesus. I know you may not feel like it; you look at your life in the earth realm and doubt, but the fact is the apostle Paul said Jesus' church rose with Him (see Eph. 2:6). It is so important for end-time revival that we know where we're seated. The church of the endtimes is going to bring revival in the earth because it's already revived, it's full, because it's seated with Christ in heavenly places. If you're already there, then you are releasing heaven from that seat. You're releasing an environment of revival on the earth. And when you do that, angels will come and join you.

ANGELS IN DREAMS

Angels' habitations are heavenly, and where they are the environments change to be like heaven. At the direction of God, angels meet us to change environments to be like God's abode, or we meet them when we choose to change our environments by faith.

Angels can show up and change things to fullness or heavenly environments in person, in a vision, or a dream. In the case of Joseph, the father of Jesus, they came through a dream portal into Joseph's mind and revealed themselves with a command from the Lord. Why? Because heaven needed a direct pathway to the earth realm to change him. Anytime the angels come and join us in our work, they're here to bring heaven to earth. They're here to change the environment on the earth. So when we talk about end-time revival, the ministry of angels is a part of that.

In the endtimes, as the church is growing in its knowledge and understanding of the ascension of Jesus Christ, it is going to become more powerful. The angelic hosts will come around and spend more time with the members of Christ's body here on the earth to do the work. The church has been working alongside angels for centuries. Ever since the beginning of time, angels have been present and they have been there to assist God in His work. But the most amazing thing is that we can participate with them for what God is doing in the earth. That is the most powerful thing to know—that we have come to that place in history. We no longer have to wait for an angel sighting. As the end-time church, we can activate our faith to change environments, angels will join us and we can also join them quicker when we know about the habitations they keep. It's exciting to know that we are positioned to work with the angels in the here and now. The church will see more signs, miracles, and wonders, and the angels will be more present in the natural realms as the end-time church becomes more activated in its positional seat of power.

KNOW ANGELS IN THE SPIRIT

Here's the deal—you can know angels in the spiritual realm long before you ever know them in the natural. Everybody wants to see the big angel in front of them, but listen—you have the capacity by faith, because you're seated with Christ in heavenly places, to experience angels every day through your spiritual senses. By faith that connection with angels is already available to you. You can already have that every moment of your life, whether or not you see the huge angel in front of you in the natural realm. The more you live in that space of faith and fullness, the more that heavenly habitation becomes part of your normal life, and the more angelic activity you'll see around you in the spirit realm. That spiritual perspective is in visions, in dreams, in the spirit realms, and even in the sense of feeling. I can not only see angels in the spirit realm, but I can also feel them in the natural realm, where there is an emotional connection. You feel the power and the presence of the angels. The angels have been with Jesus and they're with the Father all the time, around His throne. They know and sense everything about Him. They are carriers of that glory presence of God and have His anointing with them when they are dispatched into the earth realm.

Because of their close proximity to Him, you may sense their presence in the natural. You may sense guardian angels, healing angels, angels of provision or protection, fire purification angels, and all different kinds of angels. If you want to have more angelic encounters, change your mind-set. Have an ascension mind-set of fullness and you will experience more angels. With this knowledge and perspective, you won't just be waiting for angels to invade your space and begin to give you directives; you'll be able to participate with angels, just like when satan spoke to Jesus:

> *And saith unto him, If thou be the Son of God, cast thyself down: for it is written, He shall give his angels charge concerning thee: and in their hands they shall bear thee up, lest at any time thou dash thy foot against a stone* (Matthew 4:6 KJV).

That's the level of confidence we should have with angels. We should know for sure that the angels are with us at all times. Even satan knew this. We should know it more than the devil because our eyes are open to Jesus' death, burial, resurrection, and ascension. We can call on angels in an instant. That's a place of fullness, not of lack like when the angel met Joseph and had to reveal to him that there was greater fullness in faith. The revelation of God's plan for Joseph that the angel brought from heaven was for him to be the earthly father of Jesus, the Savior—this was fullness.

We are in the fullness today. You do not have to die in your body first to realize this. It is available to you now and to the church of Jesus Christ. The end-time church has gone to that place of being resurrected and ascended. Sin, death, and the grave are defeated and we are seated now as heirs of the Most High God. We have that power. We're in the fullness. Ephesians 1:3 says:

Blessed be the God and Father of our Lord Jesus Christ, who hath blessed us with all spiritual blessings in heavenly places in Christ (KJV).

Then the apostle Paul says in Ephesians 1:9-11:

Having made known unto us the mystery of his will, according to his good pleasure which he hath purposed in himself: that in the dispensation of the fulness of times he might gather together in one all things in Christ, both which are in heaven, and which are on earth; even in him: in whom also we have obtained an inheritance, being predestinated according to the purpose of him who worketh all things after the counsel of his own will (KJV).

This is a time when we are called to walk in the fullness. It is here now.

MANIFEST ANGELS IN FULLNESS

I want you to say, "I am in the fullness. I'm in the fullness." As you say, "I'm in the fullness," you're going to begin to see the manifestation of the angels coming around. You're going to begin to walk in greater confidence. You're going to start declaring, decreeing, and establishing. You're going to begin to know that you have angels with you that are there to change environments. When you know the will of the Father, you'll be able to speak His will and know that the angels are coming to assist in that. This kind of faith eradicates doubt. Doubt flees and faith enters. You will not have all these thoughts about whether or not you can see them with your natural eyes. No, just because you can't see them doesn't mean that they're not there. The devil is a liar and he flees when we exercise our faith.

Now, by faith, angels are present because you are part of a portal they're going to come through in order to impact the earth. They're coming through because of your faith, because you're a glory portal, and because you're inviting an atmosphere for them to come and gather. These are not just your guardian angels or the ones that are assigned to you, but any angel that God needs to be released for His purposes. Those angels will be there to come and help make a difference.

I just want to encourage you today. When you're having a meal with your family, all your angels are present. You start playing worship music and praise music in your house. When you begin to sing praises to the Lord and take communion together, all of a sudden your house gets flooded with angels. It becomes a habitation for angels. If there's negativity around you but you come in singing a worship song, immediately the angels come in. They enter that environment and every demonic force must flee, and the heavenly hosts take rulership. They have power over the demonic. Demonic forces can only live in the first and second heaven, which is the earth realm and the stratosphere. They do not have the authority that third-heaven angels do, and they will lose residency when the third-heaven angels show up.

To sum this up, if we want to see end-time revival, we have to have an ascension mind-set. An ascension mind-set opens us up to living in a heavenly habitation on earth because our spirit and our soul are really seated with Christ in heavenly places. That's where our spirit and soul are, yet we're actually doing the physical work of the kingdom on the earth in our body. We become a portal where heaven comes to earth through us and the angels join. If you hold fast to this truth, then you are going to see the manifestation. This is the atmosphere the church needs for end-time revival. Everybody wants to see end-time revival. When we, the church, begin to rule and reign from that position, everything opens up for us.

LIGHT AS AN ANGEL ATMOSPHERE

Now let me get a bit more practical here. Of course, worship music is an atmosphere that will invite angels. But I have also discovered from scripture and from personal experience that angels migrate to the light. The Word says in James 1:17, "Every good and perfect gift is from above, coming down from the *Father of* the heavenly *light*s, who does not change like shifting shadows."

Jesus is light. It is an attribute of the Father and Jesus. In John 8:12, the Word says of Jesus, "Then spake Jesus again unto them, saying, I am the light of the world: he that followeth me shall not walk in darkness, but shall have the light of life" (KJV). The Holy Spirit is depicted as a dove with light. Matthew 3:16 reads, "As soon as Jesus was baptized, he went up out of the water. At that moment heaven was opened, and he saw the Spirit of God descending like a dove and alighting on him."

Jesus is the light, and He had angels all around Him to the point that satan said in Matthew 4:6:

> *"If you are the Son of God," he said, "throw yourself down. For it is written: 'He will command his angels concerning you, and they will lift you up in their hands, so that you will not strike your foot against a stone.'"*

The Lord revealed to me one Christmas that angels migrate around the lights of trees and houses at Christmas time. There is a spirit of joy, thanksgiving, and peace that rests upon those who are inviting Jesus to come and be with them. He showed me that when people would celebrate Him by revealing their love through putting out lights and lighting candles then the angels would come and join them in the worship of Him. This truly is the Spirit of Christmas, and where the spirit of Christ is there are angels. Angels come to cheer on where we are and what we are doing when our hearts are for worshiping Him.

At the birth of Jesus there are lights put in cities, towns, state capitals, country monuments, churches, governmental offices, schools, you name it. We, the church, put lights to celebrate the birth of Jesus all over the world. Even in scripture we read about the importance of lights and angels during Christmas time:

> And there were shepherds living out in the fields nearby, keeping watch over their flocks at night. An angel of the Lord appeared to them, and the glory of the Lord shone around them, and they were terrified. But the angel said to them, "Do not be afraid. I bring you good news that will cause great joy for all the people. Today in the town of David a Savior has been born to you; he is the Messiah, the Lord. This will be a sign to you: You will find a baby wrapped in cloths and lying in a manger." Suddenly a great company of the heavenly host appeared with the angel, praising God and saying, "Glory to God in the highest heaven, and on earth peace to those on whom his favor rests." When the angels had left them and gone into heaven, the shepherds said to one another, "Let's go to

*Bethlehem and see this thing that has happened, which
the Lord has told us about"* (Luke 2:8-15).

People are full of joy at Christmas because they are celebrating
Jesus and the angels of joy have come to infiltrate their homes and
environments in response. When we show our love for Jesus out-
wardly, we are positioning ourselves for a release of joy.

FESTIVAL OF LIGHTS

Christmas is about Jesus and His birth. But this message of angels
being attracted to light is pertinent to the Hebrew calendar in
December also. In the month of Kislev on the Hebrew calendar,
Hanukkah, the festival of lights, occurs. It is the time for the festival of dedication:

> *Then came the Festival of Dedication at Jerusalem. It
> was winter, and Jesus was in the temple courts walking in
> Solomon's Colonnade* (John 10:22-23).

When the menorah is lit, the angels are present. Antiochus
Epiphanes, a Syrian ruler, had tried to force the Jews to abandon
their laws. He put pigs on the altar and turned it to the worship
of Zeus. Then one family, the Maccabees, led by Matthias and
his five sons fought back, and one of his sons, Judas, cleansed and
rededicated the temple. The story goes that when the priests went
in to light the menorah, there was only enough oil for one day of
burning, but miraculously it burned for eight days. Eight is a spiritual number for new beginnings. The angels were present for this
because it involved the temple and light. How do we know? By
faith. Everywhere there is a temple and light, there are angels present, sent by God to proclaim what is His and protect it.

I want you to start expecting to experience angels. The temple and light are natural elements that represent Jesus! Where Jesus is, the angels are. Where Jesus is, there is power, because He is the Word, and angels respond. Pay attention to the lights by faith, and you will begin to experience angels.

> *In the beginning was the Word, and the Word was with God, and the Word was God. He was with God in the beginning. Through him all things were made; without him nothing was made that has been made. In him was life, and that life was the light of all mankind. The light shines in the darkness, and the darkness has not overcome it* (John 1:1-5).

If you want to begin to see angels, you must first begin by faith to understand what and where angels inhabit. When we are in church services worshiping and lighting candles, the angels come to where the light is to give glory to God. We have to realize this by faith. We may not see them with natural eyes, but they are there and the more we believe the more we will see them.

ANGELS OF JOY AND LIGHT

I was visited by the joy angel one morning in my dreams. I had been struggling the night before with some anger and frustration over a recent incident in my life. I was carrying some things that I needed to lay before the Lord, but I had not done so before I went to bed. That was a sin, as apostle Paul said, "'In your anger do not sin': Do not let the sun go down while you are still angry" (Eph. 4:26).

I woke up at 3 a.m. with a severe migraine. Nothing is worse than waking up with a headache when you are supposed to be rested. I was disobedient, and my body manifested the stress I was carrying in this migraine. But the Holy Spirit moved on me in my sleep, and I began to confess my sadness and anger over this issue as I was waking up. I began to repent and ask God to forgive me for not letting this thing go. I asked Him to purify my heart of anything ungodly I was holding on to. I felt His presence and then fell back asleep, even with the headache.

It is amazing how God wanted my heart clean before Him and He helped me do it in the middle of the night. He is so good. After I returned to sleep, I was met by an angel of joy who healed me. This angel turned my lack and deficit into a complete break-through of healing and joy. I went into a deep dream state. I found myself in this dream at my parents' home in Virginia, which they bought after I became an adult. I was sitting on a bed that was actually in their living room instead of a bedroom. I looked up at the ceiling of this room and there was a white cloud forming like a galaxy. It was like the glory of Lord, and it was cotton and fluffy white and full of white feathers. As I looked closer, there were tiny angels dancing in the feather cloud galaxy and it got thicker and thicker with feathers and clouds, and then the feathers began to fall to the ground in pieces that I could pick up and touch in the dream.

Then a small angel flew out of the feather cloud galaxy formation and it flew to the left. It was translucent, so I could see through it. Then I grabbed it to touch it, and it turned into a human form of an angel about 20 inches long that almost looked like a doll with blonde hair, a white gown with blue, and peaceful big blue eyes and lashes. I was amazed at this angel's presence and I felt such overwhelming peace and joy come over me, like a child. I got my mother so I could show her, and she sat next to me on the bed in the living room and was amazed.

When I woke up from this encounter, I was filled with joy and peace and the migraine was gone completely. I got out of bed and looked at a picture that a prophetic artist in our church had given me of an angel with a trumpet that looked exactly like her. The artist had named the picture "The Angel of Joy." I had to laugh; I had encountered her personally in my dream, and here she was in a picture drawn by someone else who had seen her. Angels are usually not defined as male or female. The word *angel* in the Hebrew is *malak*, a masculine form, as is the Greek word *aggelos*. I am referring to this angel in this dream as a "she" because I have no other words to describe what I saw. The angels of joy are neither male nor female, but we often attribute human characteristics because we have no other words to describe. The thing I remember the most is that my whole countenance changed when I encountered the angel of joy in my dreams.

ANGEL SIGNET RING

The next night I had another visitation from an angel of joy. This angel owned a farm, and I was at his house riding animals. He gave me a plastic yellow signet ring with a "G" on it. He also had a matching one. We both flew together on a bike that had silver ski runner. We arrived at a Christmas village and took a picture in front of a Christmas tree. There was such joy and celebration as I felt I was home. In my own life, as I mentioned, I was feeling like a victim to some people's choices, a pawn in their world, so this encounter encouraged me to keep pressing forward and stay the course. It gave me a peace that if I remain with God in the midst of what is going on around me, I will not be concerned about man's choices as they are nothing compared to God's plans for me. Just like the bike with the ski runner, I will skate right into what God has for me.

ROOM OF VICTORY, LIGHT, AND GLORY

Later, God showed me that there is a room in His heavenly mansion that is at the back of the main mansion house. You can see it once you enter into His mansion and go to the very back of the foyer area. It is a room full of light and glory. It has a threshold with a green garland that swings under the door frame. This room has so much light that it was calling you to enter it. The garland in Greek times was worn as a crown representing victory. This is a room full of victory, light, and glory.

James 1:12 says, "Blessed is the man who endures temptation; for when he has been approved, he will receive the crown of life which the Lord has promised to those who love Him." *Crown* is the Greek word *stephanos* and is a twine or wreath often represented as a badge of royalty, a prize in public games, or symbol of honor. In ancient times this was given in the form of a wreath or garland of oak, ivy, parsley, myrtle, or olive branches. Later, these natural wreaths were imitated in gold.

This room was a room of victory or completion, and that is what it felt like as I saw it from outside the door. It was like a work had been finished and it was full of victory, love, glory, and joy.

Remember, everything in the earth realm was first created in the heavenly realms. These created things can represent Him if they are kept in their proper place in our hearts. Keep this in mind—heavenly things are made manifest on the earth, so it is heart of man that makes things deceitful, not God. Worship the Lord and serve Him only and these earthly things will not be a snare to us.

The reason I did not go in the room full of victory, love, glory, and light was because I was led to go into a writing room. This room was on the left side of the mansion house. There were angels meeting me to write this book and many others. I had to go to that place first. I believe in due time I will have the opportunity to go into the room full of victory, glory, and light, but I feel full in my heart for now that I know what is in it and I am filled with joy.

GOD IS LIGHT AND JOY

We know that the angels of light and joy are manifestations of God's very own nature. Joy is a manifestation of His Holy Spirit's presence. Read some of these scriptures below so you can see the power of the gift of joy that flows from knowing God. God has surrounded Himself with angels that reflect His very countenance.

> *But the fruit of the Spirit is love, joy, peace, longsuffering, gentleness, goodness, faith, meekness, temperance: against such there is no law* (Galatians 5:22-23 KJV).
>
> *Then he said unto them, Go your way, eat the fat, and drink the sweet, and send portions unto them for whom nothing is prepared: for this day is holy unto our Lord:*

neither be ye sorry; for the joy of the Lord is your strength
(Nehemiah 8:10 KJV).

*For the Lord shall comfort Zion: he will comfort all her
waste places; and he will make her wilderness like Eden,
and her desert like the garden of the Lord; joy and gladness shall be found therein, thanksgiving, and the voice of
melody* (Isaiah 51:3 KJV).

*A merry heart doeth good like a medicine: but a broken
spirit drieth the bones* (Proverbs 17:22 KJV).

YOUR TEMPLE BURNS BRIGHT

The angel of joy comes to pronounce who God is and bring the
joy of the Lord to certain environments. We need to learn to keep
our hearts pure and pray for the joy of the Lord to be bound to our
soul. His joy is a gift, and the angels surrounding us want us to
experience that joy because then we can stand strong. You are the
temple of the Holy Spirit, and on the inside of you burns a bright
candle light. First Corinthians 6:19-20 says:

*Do you not know that your bodies are temples of the
Holy Spirit, who is in you, whom you have received from
God? You are not your own; you were bought at a price.
Therefore honor God with your bodies.*

When you accept Jesus as Lord and Savior, the deep inside your
spirit man becomes the light of the house. The inner court of your
temple is your soul. It has pure elements of the tabernacle that are
filled with light, like the bread of His presence, the menorah or
lampstand, and the altar of incense. You should have the fullness
of His bread or life coming out your soul, the light of the menorah,

and the sweet-smelling fragrance of incense in the temple. This is who you are, technically.

Your soul is where your mind, will, and emotions reside. Emotions can emit the fruit of the Spirit mentioned in Galatians 5:22-23 above, or they can emit the darkness of unforgiveness, bitterness, hatred, impure thoughts, feelings, depression, anxiety, fear, and so on, if our souls are damaged with pain, trauma, and so on. This depends on how our soul is responding to the Spirit of God burning on the inside of us. Our body is the outer court of the temple, and in it we must remain holy. Sometimes we put our body into places we should not be, with people we should not be with, doing things we should not be doing, and this invites darkness into our souls or the inner court of our temple.

Our spirits stay holy, righteous, and bright like the blue light at the center of a flame. I will talk more about this in later chapters on color and angels, but for now know that your spirit man, with the Holy Spirit inside you, burns with a bright, silvery blue flame. This is like the Holy of Holies or the throne room of God—it is full of light. Your inner court will burn orange, yellow, and red. This light will overflow into your outer court or body. Then you give off a light from the spirit realm to the earth realm. These lights are recognized by the angelic hosts. Your guardian angels and the heavenly hosts can see your light shining. You are bright like a diamond, shining in the atmosphere. You are a heavenly habitation for angels of light to migrate toward.

Not only can we create actual environments to invite angels, we can also be the temple they choose to hang around. What kind of angels are you drawing? We give off colors into the spirit realm that attract or repel them. If we give off bright light that penetrates through our soul and body, our eyes and skin will glow—we will carry the fire of God. We will have the appearance of being a bright temple where the Holy Spirit resides, and we will attract to us the things of heaven. We can maintain this type of light by remembering our ascension seat in heavenly places. In heavenly places, you glow with this light. You are seated with Christ in the throne room where bright, silvery blue seraphim and orange, yellow, and red cherubim reside. This is the atmosphere of heaven, and if you carry this with you on earth, you are a portal for the glory and the angels will come near you and respond to your calls for helping others and serving God.

If you are not burning a light this bright out through your soul, it is overwhelmed with the sand and soot of life, and you are harboring unforgiveness, anger, hatred, and bitterness. This makes your spirit light dimmer and not able to go out of your soul and body to attract the angels of heaven. Instead, you will attract the fallen angels or demonic forces to come around you. They see you suffering and they will antagonize that. Your guardian angel is for you and will be standing with you until you cry out to God for help through your mind, will, and emotions. Until you speak and they hear the voice of God in His Word, a spark will not be lit to send them forth to help you the way you need it. I will share more about this spark of God's voice in later chapters.

So what are you attracting? As a child of God, we have His burning spirit as a blue flame inside us, but if we suffocate the flame we will be attracting the wrong spirits. Sometimes it is not our fault even if we attract these negative fallen angels—it is simply a result of being in this fallen world. They look for ways to taunt our souls because they live in the soulish realms of the earth. They prey on the trauma that has come to our souls. If you have a damaged soul and memories of horrible places and difficult things, this pain, unconfessed to God, can attract these forces. Sometimes things that we see or experience, especially at a young age, will harm us and make our souls manifest things in our bodies. God wants to heal you so your light will shine bright for Him. You are made as a temple of the Holy Spirit, and God wants you to remember your place seated with Him in heavenly places and how to operate from this place of love and forgiveness, not what you are feeling at the time.

If this is you today and you have attracted trauma, which manifests as sadness, anger, unforgiveness, bitterness, resentment, hatred, and whatever negative emotions, I want you to share that with God. He wants to cleanse your temple of impurities so you can shine bright and attract to yourself from the heavenly realms what is yours. He wants angels to migrate to you. He wants you to feel His love and presence, and theirs too, so you have confidence to call on God and know the angels will come to you. God wants a relationship with you that is pure, with no separation at all. We make the separation, but because we died, buried, were resurrected, and ascended with Jesus, this is all just an earthly thing that is overcome when we practice our heavenly seat.

PRAYER TO ENCOUNTER ANGELS OF LIGHT AND JOY

Please join me in prayer for strongholds of the enemy to be broken off your soul so your light shines big for Him.

Lord, please forgive me if I have held on to negative thoughts and emotions from my past, trauma in my soul, anger, bitterness, resentment, unforgiveness, and all types of negative emotions—fear, anxiety, depression, anger, and frustration. Thank You for sending Jesus and for cleansing my spirit when I received Him as my Savior. I know I am forgiven because of His blood. Now please cleanse my soul and the places that hurt so my inner court can shine brightly for You into my outer court, my body. I want to attract to myself the angels of light and joy. Help me apply this every day so I shine bright for You. I want my temple to reflect Your light only to this world.

Lord, help me to encounter the angels of light and joy. Father, increase my faith so I can stand on the Word of God, knowing the joy of the Lord is my strength. Lord, I bind every force that comes to lie to me and tell me that You do not love me and joy is not mine. Lord, teach me to laugh more and experience health to my bones. Reveal to me the secrets of the kingdom of heaven where joy resides in fullness. Fill my soul with Your Holy Spirit so the joy of the Lord will remain. Lord, send Your joy angels to surround me tonight and fill me with joy in Your presence. I confess anything that I am harboring in my heart that would prevent me from experiencing the joy of the Lord. Thank You, Jesus, for coming to set me free that I may experience Your joy and the presence of Your heavenly joy angels who come to bring good tidings of great joy for me today. Open my heart to experience more joy every day.

Lord, surround me with Your light—may it permeate around me so that the darkness will flee. In that encounter with Your light, I will begin to express the light and the angels will come and commune with me because they draw near to the light. Thank You for teaching me the importance of being a carrier of Your light and joy so I can experience the angels of light and joy. Also, thank You for sending them to me to help me see things from Your perspective when I am sad, fearful, or anxious. Please send them to me in dreams, visions, and in the Word of God so my faith will increase and I can participate with angels to not only be changed but to help change others.

CHAPTER 3

ANGELIC FUNCTIONS

NOW THAT YOU HAVE ACQUIRED AN ASCENSION MIND-SET, LET us begin to talk about the types of angels and how they actually function in the earth realm. You learned in the last chapter about the angels of light and joy. Angels manifest characteristics of the Father of light Himself. There are many types of angels, and in the chapters ahead we will be looking at the different kinds as they relate to the topics in each chapter.

Now, let us discover according to the Word what King Jesus actually purposes angels to do. We read in the book of Jeremiah, "Then the Lord said to me, 'You have seen well, for I am ready to perform My word'" (Jer. 1:12 NKJV). God watches over His Word and to perform it, and He sends angels to bring about the fullness of the word.

> *Bless the Lord, ye his angels, that excel in strength, that*
> *do his commandments, hearkening unto the voice of his*

word. Bless ye the Lord, all ye his hosts; ye ministers of his, that do his pleasure (Psalm 103:20-21 KJV).

One of the roles of angels is to perform the Word of God as they listen to it and respond to it. As we speak the Word, angels respond. They are ministering spirits that bring things from heaven into the earth realm at the command of God. They follow after His Word. They are where the Word is! They walked with Jesus and they walk with us because He is in us and it is His Word that we speak. Where the Word is, angels are present to perform it.

GOD COMMANDS ANGELS

Let me emphasize that God commands His angels. We don't command His angels. We speak His Word and they hearken to it. We command the Word of God and they join us in the completion and the fulfillment of the Word of God. This means speaking the Word is very important to the process of seeing angels and learning how to participate with them. If you're not soaking in the Word, you're not allowing the Word of God to transform your soul, your mind, your will, and your emotions. If you're not speaking the Word of God, then God won't release angels to come and perform the Word. When we're in need, God will send us angelic messengers. They are assigned to us to perform the commands of the King. There are so many of them and they do so many different things. Take a moment and think about things that you might need in the earth to survive. We need love, provision, strength, encouragement, healing, restoration, financial blessings—these types of things and more. Angels are on assignment to bring these things into our life. They bring them straight from heaven into earth.

TYPES OF ANGELS

So what kind of angels are there? We have seraphim and cherubim angels that have all different kinds of wingspans. There are two-winged, four-winged, and six-winged angels of prosperity, provision, and comfort. Angels of fire come for revival or healing; angels of replenishment will replenish us when we are weak or grieving. As we go through the Word of God, we see different things happening on the earth. If something can be created on the earth and managed, it needs an angel to watch over it and help bring God's plan into completion. Many times, we see angels are right there in the midst of what is happening. Hebrews 1:14 reads, "Are they not all ministering spirits, sent forth to minister for them who shall be heirs of salvation?" (KJV).

So who needs salvation? The angels don't have to be saved. We are the ones who need salvation. Man is fallen in his nature and needs a Savior. We have to receive Jesus as our Lord and Savior because we are part of fallen humanity. When we receive Jesus by asking for forgiveness of our sins and asking the Lord to come and cleanse us and heal us, we will be made brand new in our spirit man. As a brand-new spirit, you also have a soul, which includes your mind, your will, and your emotions. Your soul is being transformed daily into the likeness of Christ. Angels are sent by God so that we might have all the provision that we need in any area to accomplish the plans and purposes of God as agents in the kingdom. We need certain things, and the angels are assigned to us so that humans and angels can both be working in unity for the kingdom of God.

DEFINITION OF ANGEL

The word *angel* in the Hebrew is the word *malak*. It means to dispatch as a deputy, a messenger, or one who carries a message. It's almost like a prophet or a teacher, but this is one who is sent, who is commissioned to perform a purpose for God. God uses angels to accomplish His purpose. The Greek word for *angels* is *aggelos,* and it means "messenger" or "sent one." They are ministering spirits who are beneficent and are called to perform a public service or a religious or charitable function. They worship, they obey, and they relieve pressure—that's what ministering spirits do. They are called to administer or attend, bring official aid to us. The root Greek word *diakonos,* for the word *minister,* means "one who brings relief as in an attendant, like a waiter at a table or one who does menial duties or runs errands."

Imagine for a minute that you are seated at a table with friends and your guardian angel is there, along with the angels of many others. They're standing right next to you as you're seated around your table, fellowshipping with your friends, eating with your family—whatever that scenario looks like to you, you have angels right there. They're waiting to hear the Word of God so that they might come and perform it. So if you're sitting with your family and your friends and you began to start speaking the Word, praising God, and talking about the purposes of God, the angels then move from their waiting position. They come and begin to serve us on behalf of God.

I always have this nice picture in my head of the angels waiting with me, all the time. They're waiting for me to speak the Word so that they can come and perform it, because God says He watches to perform His Word (see Jer. 1:12). So as God is watching, the angels are waiting to come and perform the Word. This should be increasing your faith right now—you should be stepping into a place where you are beginning to believe that your guardian angel is not only there to protect you, but also to perform the Word that you speak. Knowing that your angels are always willing to participate with you should give you a sense of peace. They just need you to begin to speak the Word of God. In Psalm 91:9-16, this is what the Word reads:

> *Because thou hast made the Lord, which is my refuge, even the most High, thy habitation; there shall no evil befall thee, neither shall any plague come nigh thy dwelling. For he shall give his angels charge over thee, to keep thee in all thy ways. They shall bear thee up in their hands, lest thou dash thy foot against a stone. Thou shalt tread upon the lion and adder: the young lion and the dragon shalt thou trample under feet. Because he hath set his love upon me, therefore will I deliver him: I will set him on high, because he hath known my name. He shall call upon me, and I will answer him: I will be with him in trouble; I will deliver him, and honour him. With long life will I satisfy him, and shew him my salvation* (KJV).

Psalm 91:11-12 shows us that He will command His angels concerning us to guard us in all our ways. Yes, you have a guardian angel. I just want you to think on that for a few moments. I believe our God wants us to participate with angels and have our faith increased to the point where we make choices by faith to follow

His Word. If He has chosen to assign angels, to us then we should thank Him for those angels. I also believe it would be in the best interests of God and the kingdom if we knew the angels who are with us in the process of kingdom advancement and how best to work with them. Therefore, I would like you to join me in a prayer of thanksgiving and revelation.

PRAYER TO REVEAL GUARDIAN ANGELS

Dear Lord, thank You for assigning me an angel at conception. I would like to encounter my angel in a dream or vision or in the natural sense so that I can know who You have assigned to work with me for kingdom advancement. I know an angel is assigned to me because Your Word tells me that in Psalm 91:11. I will not pray to my angel or worship him; I just want to know how I can best participate with him. You are King of the universe and You sent Jesus to die, be buried, resurrect, and ascend so I may be forgiven of my sins and properly positioned to be a change agent in the earth. Thank You for revealing to me the heavenly being You have assigned to work alongside me for the kingdom. I stand in faith knowing that my guardian angel is watching over me night and day and that, in God's timing, I will know in my heart for sure who he is and his role in helping me on the earth. Lord, take my faith to the next level; then my eyes will open and I will be able to see what I already believe to be true by faith.

Now begin thanking and praising God for your angel.

TRACKER ANGEL

One night before going on a healing and miracle ministry trip to Ireland and England, I had a dream about one of the angels God assigned to me for a new duty. The name I gave him was Tracker Angel because I could see in the spirit realm that he was tracking my moves. In this dream, he was revealed to me. I was in a television studio and there was a man in a referee uniform, and he was recording everywhere I went and everything I did. He was also watching me on a big television screen within the television studio. He was tracking my moves. I had peace knowing he was doing this. He could keep up with me, and I was running around a lot from one scene in my television studio to another. I asked him questions too, so I knew he was an angel there to protect me and keep me on track so I would not harm myself or make wrong decisions while I was accomplishing the work of the Lord on the earth. I believe God revealed him to me in a dream before my big trip overseas so I knew there was an angel assigned to me to make sure I would make it everywhere and to increase my faith that I would accomplish God's plan on this trip.

While on my overseas trip, I would thank the Lord continually for my Tracker Angel. I was conscious that he was there helping me not to forget things, encouraging me to make my trains or airplanes and get to my hotels, and finding me places to eat, amongst many duties. I knew he was a friend with me on my travels to make sure I was getting where I needed to be. The knowledge of Tracker Angel has brought me much peace. This reminds me of the story in scripture when Jesus knew that the angels were with Him and this was confirmed by the enemy in Matthew 4:6. The angels are part of God's protection plan for us. He assigns them when we call on Him and rest in Him and His provision. Be at peace—you have a guardian angel and angels assigned for specific kingdom assignments, and God will reveal it in His time. But for now, by faith accept this as truth based on scripture.

ANGELS ENCAMP AROUND US

I'm so excited because I know your faith is increasing and you're beginning to grab hold of Psalm 91:11: "For he shall give his angels charge over thee, to keep thee in all thy ways" (KJV). You need to memorize that scripture. Here's another great scripture for you: "The angel of the Lord encamps around those who fear him, and he delivers them" (Ps. 34:7).

"Those who fear God" means "those who respect God." It doesn't mean fear as in being afraid of the Lord. It means a reverence for God. The angel of the Lord will encamp around you as you respect and revere God. And the Word tells us that God will surely deliver those who respect and revere Him. Why would an angel encamp around you for revering God? First of all, they are God's sent ones to minister to us. Also, if you respect and revere God more than the angel, God will reveal an angel to you if He knows you can handle it.

That word *encamp* in the Hebrew is the word *chanah,* which means "to pitch a tent, to abide, to set seed, or to watch." The root word is *chanan,* which means "to stoop in kindness or favor or bestow, to make lovely." This means that the angels are creating a tent to abide in. This tent is a shield of protection where kindness and favor are emitted to us. They are abiding and providing this special place of protection for us. They are watching for the Word of God so that they can go forth and perform it on God's behalf by bringing us protection.

You have an angel encamping around you right now who has set up a tent and is also a waiter, ready to wait on you when you activate him by the Word of God. I don't know about you, but that excites me a lot! That means wherever I go, there's an angel who has set up a tent of protection around me and is camping out right there waiting for me to speak the Word of God so that they can come and serve the Lord. And serving the Lord means they will also be serving me and the plan and purpose that God has for me.

An angel's job is to set up a tent or a camp. They wait and they hover. They protect our borders and they also make things lovely for us. Now, this should be a huge encouragement to you because this means that when things are bad, there's an angel that will turn it around. All you have to do is start praising the Lord and speaking the Word of God and your faith begins to increase the angels. They start moving on your behalf to make the situation a pleasant one. They protect your borders from any enemy infiltration. This is the job of the angel—it's who they are. We never have to be concerned about whether or not we're putting pressure on God to perform something because God wants to bless us and sends our angels to meet our needs for the sake of the kingdom.

God's intention is that we would be covered by protecting angels that are camping around us, waiting and protecting our borders. That brings me a lot of peace. That should bring you peace also, because no matter where you go, no matter what you're faced with, there is an angel there to help you get out of your difficult spot. These truths should also help you be more conditioned to speak in faith. When you're faced with a difficult situation, put on your faith—God comes to reward those who live by faith.

If God says my angel is here with me, I'm not going to fret. I'm not going to complain, murmur, or get upset. I'm not going to get depressed and anxious. I'm going to remember and live by faith what the Word says in Psalm 34:7 and also Psalm 91:11. I'm going to hold on to this word, and then God is going to come with His angels and perform it. There's no need to get overwhelmingly emotional about certain things because God has an angel right there waiting to step in and to bless us.

Jesus was speaking about the children and He said, "See that you do not despise one of these little ones. For I tell you that their angels in heaven always see the face of my Father in heaven" (Matt. 18:10). We know that angels are in the throne room and they see the face of the Father—all of our angels do. Whenever there's angelic activity, you will feel the holiness, the purity, the beauty, and the blessing of the Lord enveloping a room because those angels have been in the throne room. Angels have seen the face of the Father. Your guardian angel goes into realms of earth and heaven, travels between portals and sees the Father's face, and then comes back to you. You are close to the heavenly realms because your angel is present with you and your angel has been in the heavenly places with the Father. It is important for us to know we have angels assigned to us and they've seen the face of the Father in heaven.

The Lord has established his throne in heaven, and his kingdom rules over all. Praise the Lord, you his angels, you mighty ones who do his bidding, who obey his word. Praise the Lord, all his heavenly hosts, you his servants who do his will. Praise the Lord, all his works everywhere in his dominion (Psalm 103:19-22).

His angels are mighty ones who do His bidding and who obey His Word. I believe your angel right now is next to you and is doing the bidding of the Lord. The will of the Lord is to protect you, so God sent an angel on your behalf. This should increase your faith again, because this means that if God wants to see something done, His angels are going to perform it. And it's going to come when you speak the Word in faith, which will release your angel to do the will of God. Your angel is meeting your faith in God. The angels know when you believe in God's character and goodness, and this belief will be rewarded by their faithfulness to serve the Father by serving you.

FAITH DECLARATION FOR ANGELIC ACTIVITY

When we praise the Lord, all His heavenly hosts move into position to help. We are God's servants, just like the angels—we are just a different species. This is amazing. I want you to just feel the glory, the power, and the presence of God. As you know, you can be seated here with Him in this special place, knowing you are surrounded by angels right now. I am seeing the angels that are surrounding you in your room. I see you right now in the spirit realm—you are seated and you're reading this book and angels are gathering around the Word of God. Start reaching out now and touch your angel. You want to connect with your angel because your angel has been in the throne room with the Father. You are beginning to increase your faith. I see you starting to just magnify the Lord because your faith is being magnified. You're getting stronger in your spirit and in your soul. Just give Him a praise right now because the angels are coming to give you love and encouragement because that's what God wants. He wants to see you raised above that depressed state, raised out of that anxious state, and raised out of that place of worry and concern. You should have none of those because you have multiple angels waiting to perform the Word.

Just speak His Word and be praising the Lord, thanking Him and speaking that word out. Angels are at your disposal. They are dispatched by the Lord. I don't know about you, but my faith is increasing just writing this to you. Angels are with us. I'm praying right now that you are seeing them. Tell somebody—call up a friend, let somebody know because it's going to increase their faith. They're going to be able to step into the places that God has called them. Angels are on assignment, and they are surrounding you now.

PRAYER OF THANKSGIVING

I want you to say this prayer of thanksgiving and faith as God is conditioning your heart to angelic activity:

> *Lord, thank You for helping me encounter angels in this chapter and increasing my faith so that I can believe You have assigned me an angel that is protecting me, encouraging me, encamping around me with a shield of favor and blessing. Help me to continue to walk by faith in this truth so that soon I will see angels in the spirit and in the natural manifesting all around me. Lord, thank You for assigning an angel to me to protect me, to*

bring me provision from heaven, to position me for purpose and destiny. Lord, I just praise You. And I thank You right now.

My personal prayer for you as you are reading this is:

Father, I thank You for each reader because they're becoming alive in You and understanding that they have an angel. Thank You for increasing their faith and bringing them a seer anointing that they might see in the spirit, in the natural by eyes, or by their senses of smell, taste, touch, and hearing the very angel that's watching over them.

CHAPTER 4

GUARDIAN ANGELS ASSIGNED AT CONCEPTION, PART 1

W E SAID IN PREVIOUS CHAPTERS THAT GOD HAS ASSIGNED you a guardian angel. I believe you do not have just one but that you may have more than one depending on your mantle assignment. These angels watch over us daily. We have learned that God will give His angels charge over us. The scripture to remember is Psalm 91:11: "For he shall give his angels charge over thee, to keep thee in all thy ways" (KJV).

I am excited about this chapter because I am going to reveal to you that not only did you receive a guardian angel, but you received one at conception too. You see, God saw you in His mighty plan from the beginning, and He wants you to carry your destiny in the earth to completion. He has sent angels to you to help you do this. In this chapter, I want you to see the love and heart of the Father for His children. Do you know how much God loves you? You may think you do, but I tell you He loves you far more than what you can even think or imagine.

The apostle Paul shares with the Ephesian church how he hopes:

That He would grant you, according to the riches of His glory, to be strengthened with might through His Spirit in the inner man, that Christ may dwell in your hearts through faith; that you, being rooted and grounded in love, may be able to comprehend with all the saints what is the width and length and depth and height—to know the love of Christ which passes knowledge; that you may be filled with all the fullness of God. Now to Him who is able to do exceedingly abundantly above all that we ask or think, according to the power that works in us, to Him be glory in the church by Christ Jesus to all generations, forever and ever. Amen (Ephesians 3:16-21 NKJV).

My personal prayer for you today is that you grab hold of these truths and that you leave all guilt, fear, and shame behind. Jesus died, was buried, and resurrected that you might be saved, healed, and redeemed. Jesus wants a personal relationship with you and He came to make that happen. Please keep this in mind as you read this chapter. You are not a happenstance or a chance; you are God's special creation. You were in God's mind before you were born. Man's agendas cannot accomplish the heart of God, and God is bigger than our sin and the ways of the flesh. He proved this before the foundation of the world when His intention was to bring us on the scene. In this passage below in Genesis, we read God's intention before we ever came to be.

And God said, Let us make man in our image, after our
likeness: and let them have dominion over the fish of the
sea, and over the fowl of the air, and over the cattle, and
over all the earth, and over every creeping thing that
creepeth upon the earth (Genesis 1:26 KJV).

You see the Trinity—which includes the Father, Son, and Holy Spirit—were present before we were created and had roles in our creation and salvation. Jesus' role was to come to earth as the pure sacrifice for our sin. He came to reconcile us back to God and give us the keys to the kingdom so by faith we could live like we are in the Garden of Eden today.

Knowing that God has a plan for your life will give you a new perspective. He also has one for your children, whether they are alive in this earth realm or alive in the heavenly realms. Death is only an earthly thing; it has been defeated and the power of sin and the grave have been overcome by the resurrection of Jesus. This defeat of death means we have spiritual life now in the earth that affects our souls and bodies and we have spiritual life in heaven that is eternal and begins the day we accept Jesus as our Lord and Savior.

It is true—God has a plan and purpose for every child conceived, which is why He chooses to assign an angel at conception for each life on the planet. You may say, "No way, Dr. Candice, that cannot be true. The world tells me that babies are not babies until they are born." Well, that is not a truth. All babies are life at conception, which is why God sends an angel to protect them from that very point. In scripture, the truth is revealed that life on earth was planned by God and all of creation is under His rulership. In

Psalm 139:13-18, David is sharing words from God's heart for him. He says:

> *For you created my inmost being; you knit me together in my mother's womb. I praise you because I am fearfully and wonderfully made; your works are wonderful, I know that full well. My frame was not hidden from you when I was made in the secret place, when I was woven together in the depths of the earth. Your eyes saw my unformed body; all the days ordained for me were written in your book before one of them came to be. How precious to me are your thoughts, God! How vast is the sum of them! Were I to count them, they would outnumber the grains of sand—when I awake, I am still with you.*

God sees us in our mother's womb and the days of our lives are written in His book when we are still being formed. Even if these days are righteous or sinful, they are numbered; God has them written in His book, and He has a plan attached. Jesus also had a scroll written about Him that is mentioned in Psalm 40:6-8 and quoted by the author of Hebrews:

> *Therefore, when Christ came into the world, he said: "Sacrifice and offering you did not desire, but a body you prepared for me; with burnt offerings and sin offerings you were not pleased. Then I said, 'Here I am—it is written about me in the scroll—I have come to do your will, my God'"* (Hebrews 10:5-7).

The truth is that God can see the unborn, and He has written in a scroll about them to do His will on earth. Babies are watched closely by God as they hold the future of His plan. They have a destiny to assist in bringing heaven to earth. Whether your baby comes to full birth in the earth or you have a miscarriage or abortion, you need to know that every baby goes to heaven. The parents' plans and purposes for the child or lack thereof do not determine the glorious, heavenly plan God has for His conceived children.

GUARDIAN ANGELS FOR ALL

Every baby who is conceived has a guardian angel to carry them through their time on the earth for the completion of the assignment that God has for them. Every miscarried or aborted child still has a guardian angel because that guardian angel carries that child all the way to heaven. We may not see that baby's plan and purpose carried out on the earth, but it will be carried out eternally from a heavenly perspective. A conceived child has emotional ties with its parents that are fulfilling a purpose—with the mother, whether the mother wants or does not want that child, and the father who was a part of that conception. We have to realize that no matter the sinfulness of humanity, our Lord in heaven is greater and He is more than enough.

There are four specific cases in the Word of God where an angel was assigned to the baby during conception to carry out the plans and purposes of God. Let's look at two of them, starting in the very first book of the Bible for our evidence.

> *God also said to Abraham, "As for Sarai your wife, you are no longer to call her Sarai; her name will be Sarah. I will bless her and will surely give you a son by her. I will bless her so that she will be the mother of nations; kings of*

peoples will come from her." Abraham fell facedown; he laughed and said to himself, "Will a son be born to a man a hundred years old? Will Sarah bear a child at the age of ninety?" And Abraham said to God, "If only Ishmael might live under your blessing!" Then God said, "Yes, but your wife Sarah will bear you a son, and you will call him Isaac. I will establish my covenant with him as an everlasting covenant for his descendants after him" (Genesis 17:15-19).

God speaks to Abraham and Sarah about the conception and birth of a promised child named Isaac. In later scriptures, we read much about the seed of this promised child, which is Jesus (see Gal. 3:29). God even established a covenant with Isaac: "But my covenant I will establish with Isaac, whom Sarah will bear to you by this time next year" (Gen. 17:21). Then, in the next chapter of Genesis, we see Abraham being visited by three men who were angels to reveal the will of God.

The Lord appeared to Abraham near the great trees of Mamre while he was sitting at the entrance to his tent in the heat of the day. Abraham looked up and saw three men standing nearby. When he saw them, he hurried from the entrance of his tent to meet them and bowed low to the ground. He said, "If I have found favor in your eyes, my lord, do not pass your servant by. Let a little water be brought, and then you may all wash your feet and rest under this tree. Let me get you something to eat, so you can be refreshed and then go on your way—now that you have come to your servant." "Very well," they answered, *"do as you say."* *So Abraham hurried into the tent to Sarah* (Genesis 18:1-6).

Then the angels inquired where Sarah was and began to prophesy over a child who was not even born yet. God knows babies and He knows conception, and He has plans. He sends His angels to make sure things take place. In Genesis 18:10-15 the angel says:

"I will surely return to you about this time next year, and Sarah your wife will have a son." *Now Sarah was listening at the entrance to the tent, which was behind him. Abraham and Sarah were already very old, and Sarah was past the age of childbearing. So Sarah laughed to herself as she thought, "After I am worn out and my lord is old, will I now have this pleasure?" Then the Lord said to Abraham, "Why did Sarah laugh and say, 'Will I really have a child, now that I am old?' Is anything too hard for the Lord? I will return to you at the appointed time next year, and Sarah will have a son." Sarah was afraid, so she lied and said, "I did not laugh." But he said, "Yes, you did laugh."*

Abraham and Sarah named their baby *Isaac* or *Yishaq*, which means "he laughs." In an earlier passage of scripture, Sarai gave her maidservant Hagar to Abram when she thought she could not conceive. Hagar became pregnant and Sarai mistreated her, so Hagar left and fled to the desert and was met by an angel who prophesied God's plan for the baby in her womb.

Then the angel of the Lord told her, "Go back to your mistress and submit to her." The angel added, "I will increase your descendants so much that they will be too numerous to count. ...You are now pregnant and you will give birth to a son. You shall name him Ishmael, for the Lord has heard of your misery. He will be a wild donkey of a man; his hand will be against everyone and everyone's hand against him, and he will live in hostility toward all his brothers." She gave this name to the Lord who spoke to her: "You are the God who sees me," for she said, "I have now seen the One who sees me." That is why the well was called Beer Lahai Roi; it is still there, between Kadesh and Bered (Genesis 16:9-14).

Let us examine how at conception both of these women had angels assigned to them to come and meet with them and encounter them and speak of what was currently happening and what was to come. They had angel appearances during their time of conception. God knew the fathers, the mothers, and the babies, their names, and the covenants He would make with them. Not only did they have angelic encounters during early pregnancy, or even before, in the case of Sarah, but God had sent angels to tell them what was to be; He had assigned angels to protect what He said. The Word of God was preserved by the angels so God could come and perform it. If God gave these people angels to protect them and their babies, He will do the same for us. We are not alone, and He loves us and our children. He has assigned an angel to help carry a baby to the place He has prepared for them.

THE FATHER'S LOVE

You may be thinking, "Then why do babies die? If God has a plan, why are there miscarriages and abortions?" These are good questions that I will answer in the next chapter. I realize this teaching may rock some worldviews, especially if you never thought a baby in a womb could have an angel watching over it. We will look at more scriptures in the next chapter.

For now, let us open our hearts to what we learn in the scriptures and open our minds to angel encounters. Let us believe in the goodness and love of God. First John 4:16 states, "God is love." This means love is being carried to our children. The Father's love is surrounding our children. I want you to just think on this. I know you are an adult, but you are God's very own child, so your angel is carrying God's love to you, just as he is to your children. God loves us that much—He assigns an angel to protect us, and that angel sees the face of the Father and is there to bind us to the love of God and not separate us. The Word in Romans 8:35-39 says:

> *Who shall separate us from the love of Christ? Shall trouble or hardship or persecution or famine or nakedness or danger or sword? As it is written: "For your sake we face death all day long; we are considered as sheep to be slaughtered." No, in all these things we are more than conquerors through him who loved us. For I am convinced that neither death nor life, neither angels nor demons, neither the present nor the future, nor any powers, neither height nor depth, nor anything else in all creation, will be able to separate us from the love of God that is in Christ Jesus our Lord.*

So nothing can separate us, and nothing can separate you or your baby from God's love through His assigned angel. The angels help bind us to His love and help to perform God's Word over the babies (see Jer. 1:14).

PRAYER FOR UNDERSTANDING GOD'S LOVE

Lord, please continue to reveal Your love in these chapters and show us that You have assigned an angel to us at conception to carry us through this life and into eternity. Any worldly thinking and lies of the enemy concerning these truths, I ask You to wash off the reader right now so that they would experience Your love. Bring revelation to us so we know that each of us is very important to You and there is a plan for our lives from conception forth. Reveal any lies we may be harboring so we can let them go and we can repent and begin to increase our faith in what we cannot see. We hold fast the confession of our faith as we believe in Your love and goodness and Your desire to be in relationship with humanity, so much so that You sent Jesus as the sacrificial lamb to make a way for this. Speak to us as we continue to learn and grow in an understanding of angels being assigned to us at conception.

CHAPTER 5

GUARDIAN ANGELS ASSIGNED AT CONCEPTION, PART 2

I N THIS CHAPTER, I WANT TO CONTINUE THE TOPIC OF ANGELS being assigned to us at conception. In Matthew 18:10, the Word reads, "See that you do not despise one of these little ones. For I tell you that their angels in heaven always see the face of my Father in heaven."

The angels in heaven surrounding God's throne are assigned to children. Your children's angels always see the face of God. This word *always* is the Greek word *dia,* which means "a channel of an act." They are carrying the Father's heart to the children. These angels are an extension of God's will for His children. They are agents sent by God to carry His countenance to the children. Please keep this in mind for yourself and your own children. Maybe you are someone who had to deal with a miscarriage and you desperately wanted your child, or maybe you had a difficult personal decision where you felt you had to make the choice to abort your baby. No matter which category you find yourself in, know this—God loves you and He loves your baby and He has them in His hands.

MY BABY TESTIMONY

Let me share some personal stories of three miscarriages that my husband and I had to recover from. I say both of us—we both experienced the miscarriages differently and processed them differently, but these babies belonged to both of us. It was in the year of 1992; I very much wanted to have children, and it was difficult for me. I had some fertility issues and I was on fertility medication. When I got pregnant the very first time, my husband Adam and I were delighted. At about nine weeks, the baby's heart stopped beating. I did not know this until I went in for a baby check-up appointment—the baby had passed away.

We were so heartbroken because we had waited for two years to have a child. We grieved the loss. When you really want the baby and you have a miscarriage, you grieve because of the loss of the dream. Death kills our dreams; it kills hope and a future. It was a real loss to me, as it is to all parents. I had a soul tie with this baby. After my miscarriage as I was grieving, I sought the Lord's heart on the matter because I did not understand why. No one ever knows why, but we can go to the Father and ask. I felt the Lord lead me to a book about grieving the loss of a baby, and it said that I can name my baby. I did not even know if this was biblical or not. But I believed in life after death and that Jesus made a way, so my baby must still be alive, just not here on earth.

I asked the Lord one day in prayer the name of my baby. I heard the Lord speak to me the name "Angela." I was like, "Oh my gosh, I was going to have a girl and her name's Angela." Then I looked up the name Angela, because I knew that God had spoken to me and I wanted to know what the name Angela meant. Sure enough, it was a derivative of the word *angel*, which means "messenger of God." I knew that Holy Spirit and the angels were speaking to me about Angela and that they were carrying this message to me that I would see her again. That gave me great peace.

Six months later, I got pregnant again. We were very delighted. This time, about six weeks after conception I started bleeding. I knew I was miscarrying again. But this time it was different, because I stopped bleeding after a while and started again ten days later. I sought the Lord on this for the baby's name again. He said, "Thomas." I looked up the meaning of that baby name, and it means "twin." I had bled two separate times over about a two-week period of time. God was telling me the babies were two boys and not one. I just believed by faith that their names were Thomas 1 and 2. I believe our boys are in heaven and that I will see them again. They're with Angela and with my family who have already crossed over to heaven.

My testimony is an experience grounded on the faith that Jesus' death, burial, and resurrection made a way for me and my family to spend eternity in heaven. I have a relationship with the Father because of the Son, Jesus, and His atoning sacrifice for my sin. I know God will speak in His Word and other supernatural ways. God loves me, He loves you, and He wants those who seek His face to see heaven and know more of His love.

NAME YOUR BABY

For those families who are suffering the loss of a child through a miscarriage or abortion, God has a name for your baby because your baby is alive. Know this—you will see your baby when you arrive in heaven. Maybe you already named your baby, but if you have not, I want to encourage you today that God will speak to you about the name of your child. God has a name for your baby, and the angels in heaven and your deceased family members and others are going to raise your children. When you get to heaven, you will see your children and they will know who you are. They are living now and they will be living when you arrive. If you would like to know the name of your baby, get into that private place and ask the Lord to reveal it to you.

It's very important that you recognize that even though you may be in the temporal realm, if you know Jesus Christ as your Lord and Savior, you are really a creature of eternity. Your babies are living in the eternal realm right now, and you are also in the eternal realm. Your body just hasn't passed away yet, but your spirit and your soul can be there while your body is on earth because of the death, burial, resurrection, and ascension of Jesus. You are seated with Him in heavenly places. Your children are in that heavenly realm now. We give all praise and glory to the Lord for the fact that our children are there in that heavenly place with Him, fulfilling their purpose. If you are dealing with grief and sorrow from your miscarriage or abortion, I just want you to know that you can have an eternal perspective, even in the pain of death, because of what Jesus Christ has done.

LOVED US FIRST

God has my babies and God has your babies. An angel was assigned to my children and your children—your aborted children, your miscarried children, and your children who have passed away. These assigned angels carried them to safe places in heaven. Exodus 23:20 reads, "See, I am sending an angel ahead of you to guard you along the way and to bring you to the place I have prepared." There is a plan and a purpose. Some carry that out on earth. Some carry that out directly in heaven. No matter what, your baby is carrying out his or her plan and purpose, and you were a vital part of that.

I believe in the love and grace of God. His love surpasses all understanding and covers a multitude of sin (see 1 Pet. 4:8). He created us for fellowship and has a plan and purpose for me and for you too. This kind of love, revealed in the Word of God, shows all of us that wherever judgment was to come upon us, instead the love of the Father prevailed through Jesus' submission to the cross. First John reveals this love of God:

> *This is how God showed his love among us: He sent his one and only Son into the world that we might live through him. This is love: not that we loved God, but that he loved us and sent his Son as an atoning sacrifice for our sins. Dear friends, since God so loved us, we also ought to love one another. No one has ever seen God; but if we love one another, God lives in us and his love is made complete in us. This is how we know that we live in him and he in us: He has given us of his Spirit. And we have seen and testify that the Father has sent his Son*

to be the Savior of the world. If anyone acknowledges that Jesus is the Son of God, God lives in them and they in God. And so we know and rely on the love God has for us. God is love. Whoever lives in love lives in God, and God in them. This is how love is made complete among us so that we will have confidence on the day of judgment: In this world we are like Jesus. There is no fear in love. But perfect love drives out fear, because fear has to do with punishment (1 John 4:9-18).

I have shared all this so that you may rest in the love of God, and the confidence of knowing God will cause all things to work for the good of those who love Him and are called according to His purpose. Judgment went on the cross. We are positioned now to be loved.

PRAYERS FOR HEAVENLY PERSPECTIVE

I would like you to pray with me to shift your perspective to eternity so that you would know that your babies are there and that you can talk to the Lord about your children. He loves children. He made a way for your children, and the angels are a very big part of that.

If your story is one of grief, loss, guilt, or condemnation from miscarriage, abortion, or death of a child, make sure you forgive yourself and receive the love of Jesus and position yourself to know that God has a plan and the angels helped carry your baby to safety. If your story is one of grief due to a miscarriage or death of a child and you are angry with God because He did not save your baby from physical death, then I want you to confess your anger toward God because it is keeping you isolated from His love. The enemy uses our trauma to hide the love of the Father from us. Tell the Lord you forgive Him for your baby's physical death and ask Him to forgive you for holding Him responsible. I realize this is intense, but when we lose a person in our life—whether it be a baby, a spouse, a family member, or a friend—we often hold God responsible because we know He could stop it and He didn't for whatever reason. The enemy wants to hold us in that place of bondage, but you must be set free. Confess where you are with the pain in your heart, and release it God. If your story is one of abortion, and you have not yet done so, take the time to ask the Lord for forgiveness and share your heart with Him. This will break off strongholds that the enemy has to your soul. God loves us and He forgives us when we repent, but we must recognize our choices and ask Him for forgiveness so purification of our souls and a new start can begin. He has assigned angels to minister healing to us, and when we do this it dispatches them to help us. I know someone is getting free right now. Pray this prayer with me:

> *Lord Jesus, please forgive me if I have not known Your true love for me, even from conception. Forgive me for any choices or decisions not in line with Your will for my life. Forgive me for holding You responsible for any pain I am experiencing. You have a great plan and purpose for me and want me to carry that on the earth. I entrust myself, my family, my children to Your care. No one can love me more or care more for me. Thank You for lifting me up so that I would not cut my foot on a stone. I surrender to You during this time—use me for Your glory. Lord, please heal my soul ties and soul wounds and*

enable me to start fresh with a new perspective of Your
love for me through the fact You sent Jesus to die, bury,
resurrect and ascend. I want to live my life in Your love
and peace. In Your name I pray, Amen.

BEFORE YOU WERE BORN

Let's focus on God's plan for you and for your children. We know
the prophet Jeremiah heard God's plan for him when He said in
Jeremiah 1:4-5:

> *Then the word of the Lord came to me, saying: "Before*
> *I formed you in the womb I knew you; before you were*
> *born I sanctified you; I ordained you a prophet to the*
> *nations"* (NKJV).

God knew Jeremiah before He formed him in his mother's
womb. Notice how God takes credit for the forming, not man.
God personally prophesied to me the conception of my oldest
daughter, Alexandria. She is the first child who came to term on
the earth after Angela and Thomases (twins).

MIRACLE STORY

God spoke to me about my new pregnancy months before it ever
happened. I believe this story will encourage you. God has every
child planned before any of them come to be. In 1993, a year
after my miscarriages, I took a job as a makeup sales consultant
for Elizabeth Arden at Gayfers Department Store in Jacksonville,
Florida. Although my first degree was a Bachelor of Business
Administration in accounting, I wanted to do something with

helping people in sales. In the fall of 1993, Elizabeth Arden ran a sales contest. It was called Dream Vacation, and if you sold a certain amount of makeup over a six-month period of time, you would have an opportunity to go on a trip to Hawaii. Hawaii was where I met my husband back in 1989, so Hawaii was a special state for us.

My manager at the Elizabeth Arden counter really wanted the trip also. The Holy Spirit fell on me and I just began to prophesy and say, "I'm going to win this trip to Hawaii and I'm going to come back with a baby." Sure enough, every day that I was working at the sales counter, people would come in and they would come straight to my counter and buy product. There were a lot of makeup counters to choose from, but they would come straight up to my counter and they would buy from us. The other sales ladies wondered, "What in the world is going on? How come they go straight to you?"

And I said, "I told you, I'm going to win this trip and I'm going to come back with a baby." Six months went by, and we had the highest sales volume in pretty much all the stores in the Jacksonville area. We were recognized on a national level, and we won the trip. Adam and I went on the Dream Vacation to Maui for an entire week, all expenses paid. The first night in Hawaii, I got pregnant with our oldest daughter, Alexandria.

You can imagine I was concerned about the pregnancy as I had lost three babies already. I prayed all the time for this baby's safety in my womb. When I was six months pregnant, my husband was approached by a new admiral to be his aide to Iceland. I was nervous about leaving the United States and going to Iceland when I knew the baby would be born there. God gave me a supernatural encounter where He revealed to me that I should go.

In order to calm my concern, my husband wanted me to talk to the current admiral's aide in Iceland and ask questions about the Keflavik Naval Hospital. The minute I heard the voice of this aide, I immediately knew I had been here before in a dream. At that moment, I knew we had to go—we had to take the leap of faith.

Even with the three prior miscarriages, the Navy authorized me to go to Iceland with my husband at six months pregnant. I went, and about 30 weeks into the pregnancy I started having early contractions. I ended up in a hospital in Reykjavik, Iceland. They did not have the same system of medicine as the United States of America, so it was a very different experience. I shared a room with five women, but again the Lord was gracious to me. I could not speak Icelandic or Dutch, so I prayed and asked the Lord for an English-speaking roommate. Miraculously, every time the bed next to me was empty, a new woman came who was English-speaking. God was with me; it was truly a blessing. I was there in the hospital for about ten days. Then the contractions stopped and I was released back to the Keflavik naval base.

Alexandria decided to come into the earth at 37 weeks and five days, on a very snowy, blustery night in Keflavik. My daughter's arrival was very purposeful in this season. It was hard for me after having left sunny Florida. I love Florida, and we had built a brand-new house there. Here I found myself in Iceland, in a tiny little apartment where it was dark 20 hours a day. Alexandria gave me a reason to live. Every day I would get up and care for her. She was a lifesaver as my husband was very busy flying all over Europe with the admiral. My baby Alex helped save me.

Then, before we even left Iceland to come back to the United States, I found I was pregnant with our son Nicholas. When Nicholas was only seven months old, I became pregnant with Samantha. Those are my three children alive in the earth realm, and Angela and Thomases (twins) are alive in the heavenly realms. It will not be long before we're all a family again.

SCRIPTURAL EXAMPLES

Rebekah also wanted children, and God had a purpose for her to have two children in her womb. God's plan starts at conception with an angel assignment to help carry the baby to purpose. God spoke to Rebekah about her twin boys in Genesis 25:21-23:

> *Isaac prayed to the Lord on behalf of his wife, because she was childless. The Lord answered his prayer, and his wife Rebekah became pregnant. The babies jostled each other within her, and she said, "Why is this happening to me?" So she went to inquire of the Lord. The Lord said to her, "Two nations are in your womb, and two peoples from within you will be separated; one people will be stronger than the other, and the older will serve the younger."*

God will speak to you directly about your babies, and He will even answer your questions when you inquire of Him. God has a destiny, plan, and purpose for all of us, and He loves us enough to talk to us about it.

We also read about another angel encounter that happened to Zechariah when he encountered the archangel Gabriel, who prophesied the birth of John the Baptist:

Then an angel of the Lord appeared to him, standing at the right side of the altar of incense. When Zechariah saw him, he was startled and was gripped with fear. But the angel said to him: "Do not be afraid, Zechariah; your prayer has been heard. Your wife Elizabeth will bear you a son, and you are to call him John. He will be a joy and delight to you, and many will rejoice because of his birth, for he will be great in the sight of the Lord. He is never to take wine or other fermented drink, and he will be filled with the Holy Spirit even before he is born. He will bring back many of the people of Israel to the Lord their God. And he will go on before the Lord, in the spirit and power of Elijah, to turn the hearts of the parents to their children and the disobedient to the wisdom of the righteous—to make ready a people prepared for the Lord." Zechariah asked the angel, "How can I be sure of this? I am an old man and my wife is well along in years." The angel said to him, "I am Gabriel. I stand in the presence of God, and I have been sent to speak to you and to tell you this good news" (Luke 1:11-19).

Mary, the mother of Jesus, had an angel encounter with Gabriel also. These angel encounters are also angel assignments to chart the course of God and bring to completion the prophecy about each one. In Luke 1:26-38 we read:

In the sixth month of Elizabeth's pregnancy, God sent the angel Gabriel to Nazareth, a town in Galilee, to a virgin pledged to be married to a man named Joseph, a descendant of David. The virgin's name was Mary.

The angel went to her and said, "Greetings, you who are highly favored! The Lord is with you." Mary was greatly troubled at his words and wondered what kind of greeting this might be. But the angel said to her, "Do not be afraid, Mary; you have found favor with God. You will conceive and give birth to a son, and you are to call him Jesus. He will be great and will be called the Son of the Most High. The Lord God will give him the throne of his father David, and he will reign over Jacob's descendants forever; his kingdom will never end." "How will this be," Mary asked the angel, "since I am a virgin?" The angel answered, "The Holy Spirit will come on you, and the power of the Most High will overshadow you. So the holy one to be born will be called the Son of God. Even Elizabeth your relative is going to have a child in her old age, and she who was said to be unable to conceive is in her sixth month. For no word from God will ever fail." "I am the Lord's servant," Mary answered. "May your word to me be fulfilled." Then the angel left her.

Then Mary went to meet Elizabeth, her cousin, who was married to Zechariah and pregnant with John. This story reveals how the baby in the womb can confirm the plan and purpose of God. Both baby Jesus and baby John gave early confirmations of the purposes of God.

At that time Mary got ready and hurried to a town in the hill country of Judea, where she entered Zechariah's home and greeted Elizabeth. When Elizabeth heard Mary's greeting, the baby leaped in her womb, and Elizabeth was filled with the Holy Spirit. In a loud voice she exclaimed: "Blessed are you among women, and blessed is the child you will bear! But why am I so favored, that the mother of my Lord should come to me? As soon as the sound of your greeting reached my ears, the baby in my womb leaped for joy. Blessed is she who has believed that the Lord would fulfill his promises to her!" (Luke 1:39-45)

The baby in the womb of Elizabeth had ears for the Savior because he had an assignment. Angels were present to make sure God's Word came to pass. In Jeremiah 1:12, the Lord spoke to Jeremiah and asked what he saw. Then the Lord said to him, "You have seen correctly, for I am watching to see that my word is fulfilled." God watches to perform His Word and make it happen with the help of angels. Angels carry us to our kingdom assignments from conception.

In Exodus 23:20-23, the Word tells us that God spoke to the nation of Israel and said:

See, I am sending an angel ahead of you to guard you along the way and to bring you to the place I have prepared. Pay attention to him and listen to what he says. Do not rebel against him; he will not forgive your rebellion, since my Name is in him. If you listen carefully to what he says and do all that I say, I will be an enemy to your enemies and will oppose those who oppose you. My angel will go ahead of you and bring you into the land of the Amorites, Hittites, Perizzites, Canaanites, Hivites and Jebusites, and I will wipe them out.

God seals His plan for you with an angel to bring it to pass. This passage of scripture is so important because it shows how God uses the angelic hosts to help carry us into destiny.

PRAYERS FOR ANGELS TO CARRY US

Join me in prayer as we ask the Lord to solidify what we learned in this chapter and help us to realize our importance to God and the importance of our children.

> *Lord, thank You for bringing me to this new knowledge and understanding of how You assigned an angel to me at conception. You have loved me from before the foundation of the world and You wanted me to be part of Your global kingdom plan. Thank You for loving me enough to send Jesus Christ to die, be buried, resurrect, and ascend for me. You have positioned me for destiny from my ascension seat in the heavenly realms, and it is here that I will carry forth Your plan and purpose. Thank You for sending the angels to encamp around me and protect me as we journey on to destiny together. Please continue to give me greater revelation about the angels and how I am to work alongside them to make changes in the world. Please make me consciously aware of the power of angels and how they manifest on the earth today. I want to partner with You and them to make a difference.*

CHAPTER 6

ANGELS OF FIRE

I N THE UPCOMING CHAPTERS WE ARE GOING TO EXPLORE THE power of the angels of fire. All angels carry fire with them, so they are all ministers of flames of fires, but there are some species that we will highlight in the next few chapters. Yes, fire angels are all around you daily. Your guardian angel is a type of fire angel, but there are some angels of fire that carry out duties that your guardian angel does not carry out. In these chapters we will be discussing those.

One of my favorite varieties of fire angels is healing fire angels. They are present in my ministry meetings. It's truly amazing to see them in activation. You might say, "What's a fire angel?" When we know and understand fire angels and how they work, we can begin to participate with them for healing and for revival. Their basic function is to bring fire from heaven to earth. Often in scripture, prophets work alongside the supernatural for fire to come into the earth.

I want to start off with Hebrews 1:7: "In speaking of the angels he says, 'He makes his angels spirits, and his servants flames of fire.'" So angels are flames of fire, and they activate healing. They fight battles; they bring revival. They are present when the intensity of Holy Spirit power is evident in meetings and people are being baptized in the Holy Spirit, among other things.

YAH-RED ANGEL

I want to tell you a little bit of a story about myself and my angels. I shared in an earlier chapter about Tracker Angel, one of my guardian angels who was revealed to me before traveling. I was also made aware, around the same time, of another one of my guardian angels assigned to help me accomplish kingdom duties. When the Lord began to call me to travel into other countries to bring the gospel, I had a dream encounter with this angel. The anointing on my life was being advanced to another level. I had always walked in healing, but my miracle ministry was not as prevalent. God had been revealing more to me about this ministry, and when He called me to travel internationally and to do healings and miracles, specifically in Ireland and England, He assigned me not just Tracker Angel but Yah-Red, the giant killer. Although I shared about Tracker Angel first in this book, it was Yah-Red who came first to me in a dream; Tracker Angel was a few months later.

One night I had a dream, and I saw this huge angel, and I was very close with this angel. We had a very intensive bond. I could feel the bond in the dream. It was very emotional, and this angel was very large, eight feet tall, and was male with flaming red hair and very white skin. He was in human form, not dressed like I would expect an angel to be dressed—he wore a blue shirt in almost a western style with jeans. I knew this was an angel. I believe his attire of blue was representative of the blue fire angels of God. The western style represented a type of cowboy or warrior figure. When I woke up from the dream, I was moved by the Spirit of God. I was very emotional. I could relive the moment in a second. It had been burned into my brain. As soon as I closed my eyes, I could see myself standing with this angel who was speaking to me and giving me orders in the dream.

This happened as I was getting ready to be launched in international ministry. I was overwhelmed. I began to investigate angels as a result of this encounter. I began to talk to some of my prophetic friends. They felt that this particular angel had been assigned to me because I was going overseas. He was a giant killer—one that would kill giants so that healings and miracles would come in the meetings. The angel actually had red hair, and I didn't totally understand what the red hair was for, but I knew that I was going to be ministering in European countries like Ireland and the United Kingdom, where red hair is a more prominent feature than in other parts of the world. It was only after I went to France that the Lord really began to show me that the red hair represented fire angels and the region; it was a twofold message.

Yah-Red was the name I heard in the dream. I wanted to find this in scripture. What I discovered was that the name Yah-Red was broken down into two words in the Bible. *Yah* or *Jah* is in the Hebrew word *Yahweh*, which is the holy name of God. It alludes to His faithfulness and the characteristics of who He is. The Jewish people don't even say *Yahweh*; they say *Ha-Shem* or *Adonai*. We see this root word, the sacred name of the Lord, in Genesis 2:4:

This is the account of the heavens and the earth when they were created, in the day that the Lord [Yehovah or Jehovah, containing Yah or Jah] *God made earth and heaven* (NASB).

The color red in Hebrew is the word *admoniy*, which means "reddish." The root word, *adam*, means "to show blood." This word *admoniy* is used of David's appearance. In this passage, David is being anointed by Samuel to be king one day, and David is in the line of Jesus.

So he sent word and brought him in. Now he was reddish, with beautiful eyes and a handsome appearance. And the Lord said, "Arise, anoint him; for this is he" (1 Samuel 16:12 NASB).

The word *reddish* is also in these scriptures below:

Then the Philistine came and approached David, with the shield-bearer in front of him. When the Philistine looked and saw David, he was contemptuous of him; for he was only a youth, and reddish, with a handsome appearance (1 Samuel 17:41-42 NASB).

Not only was David of a *reddish* appearance but he was also a giant killer.

The Philistine also said to David, "Come to me, and I will give your flesh to the birds of the sky and the wild animals." But David said to the Philistine, "You come to me with a sword, a spear, and a saber, but I come to you in the name of the Lord of armies, the God of the armies of Israel, whom you have defied. This day the Lord will hand you over to me, and I will strike you and remove your head from you. Then I will give the dead bodies of the army of the Philistines this day to the birds of the sky and the wild animals of the earth, so that all the earth may know that there is a God in Israel, and that this entire assembly may know that the Lord does not save by sword or by spear; for the battle is the Lord's, and He will hand you over to us!" (1 Samuel 17:44-47 NASB)

Then as the story continues:

So David prevailed over the Philistine with the sling and the stone: he struck the Philistine and killed him, and there was no sword in David's hand. Then David ran and stood over the Philistine, and took his sword and drew it out of its sheath and finished him, and cut off his head with it. When the Philistines saw that their champion was dead, they fled (1 Samuel 17:50-51 NASB).

The amazing things about these scriptures is that they show this "reddish" young man defeating a giant—a Philistine. At the time I had the dream, this angel was huge, like a giant with red hair. The Lord gave me the name *Yah-Red*, but I had no idea what this meant. I just knew what I saw. I do believe Yah-Red, the giant killer fire angel, is with me. I have seen miracles where giants were holding people in bondage, infirmity, sickness, and disease, but God used him in the spirit realm to kill the giants. When Yah-Red shows up, these demons are crushed and people are healed. I have seen blind eyes open and deaf ears hear, among other miracles.

In Isaiah 1:18, red is also a reference to the blood of Jesus. This fire angel, Yah-Red, had the fire properties of the Lord Himself.

"Come now, and let us debate your case," says the Lord, "though your sins are as scarlet, they shall become as white as snow; though they are red like crimson, they shall be like wool" (NASB).

We are washed in the blood of the Lamb. Ephesians 1:7 says, "In him we have redemption through his blood, the forgiveness of sins, in accordance with the riches of God's grace" (NIV). The red also represents the New Covenant, and the fulfillment of the Old Covenant because of the shed blood of the Passover Lamb, Jesus Christ. This is how the end-times angelic activity will be made manifest, through the power of the New Covenant blood of the Lamb that releases the supernatural to invade the natural with signs, miracles, and wonders by faith.

FIRE ANGELS IN FRANCE

It was only after I had been to France that the Lord really began to show me that the red hair not only represented European regions but also the power of the presence of fire angels. While I was in France, I had an amazing encounter with God. I was there doing a new revival meeting, and the fire angels showed up. When the fire angels were there, I began to sense a lot of heat in my hands and feet, kind of prickly, almost like my hands and feet had gone numb. People started to feel the temperature rising in the room. Sometimes people would say that they smelled sulfur or burning smells. I have never smelled that myself, but I do know other spiritual leaders who have said this when the fire angels are evident. We will discuss the relevance of sulfur more later and the type of fire angels that carry sulfur. Sulfur is a purifying agent around the throne of God.

Personally, I recognize fire angels from this amazing burning sensation and heat coming into the room when they are present. This began on my trip to France, and the people around started to really feel the glory fire. They would receive the baptism of Holy Spirit and healings of all kinds. There was a lot of power in the house. One time the Holy Spirit said to me, "Ask them if they want to experience the angels of fire for themselves." Then He said, "Invite them to come up front to receive healing power in their hands and to lay hands on others to see the power in action."

I was like, "OK, Lord!" I knew God was going to show up with these angels. His presence was strong and our faith was high. I said, "OK, if you have gifts of healing or if you've never received a gift of healing but you would like to receive one, I want to invite you to come up to the front." At first, I allowed God just to minister words of knowledge to people. The Holy Spirit started speaking words of knowledge. There was also an impartation of fire that was coming upon the people to receive healing gifts. The clear manifestation was that their hands and feet started to burn.

Also, people in the room were receiving healings and they weren't even being touched. This was clearly the glory of God with the activity of the fire angels. Then I instructed people to begin laying hands on others who were in pain or needed to have a healing. Then I called up another group of people who wanted to receive an impartation for healing. Once they received impartation, I asked others who needed healing to come forth to receive. Those who received the healing impartation began to lay hands on this group, and these people were healed.

There was healing in the room without laying on of hands, but there was also healing with laying on of hands. People who had never laid hands on anyone or ever walked in healing gifts were now walking in them. God did a whole session on angels while I was there in France because people began to experience them and they had a lot of questions. The glory angels came in as well, and the glory oil was being released and people were beginning to just feel the joy of the Lord. They were beginning to laugh and they felt the love of God upon them.

In the second meeting in France that I did, the glory of the Lord and joy angels came in so much that the oil of gladness was being poured over everyone. People were falling out in the glory and in the joy of the Lord. There were pockets of the glory in the house where angels were. People would stand there and fall out and laugh and cry in joy. God was healing and bringing breakthrough. These glory angels that bring oil from the vats of heaven are still a species of fire angels. All angels have fire attached to them. Stay with me as I explain more.

ANGELS OF BLUE FIRE AND GLORY

When we understand fire angels and how they work, we can begin to participate with them for healing and for revival. Their basic function is to bring fire from heaven to earth. I want to read Hebrews 1:7 again: "In speaking of the angels he says, 'He makes his angels spirits, and his servants flames of fire.'" So angels are spirits from heaven, and they are flames of fire. Now, all species of angels have some elements of fire, but there are specific types.

One of the beautiful ways I engage with the Holy Spirit is being a researcher. He takes me on journeys to mine for treasure in His Word that is useful to help others live godly and prosperous lives. The things of earth actually prove the existence of the supernatural realms. These journeys enable me to share amazing revelations with others. These revelations from heaven are being released so we can learn more about God, who He is, who He created us to be, and how He sent Jesus to save us. The angels are part of His great plan, as we are.

This is not a theology book on angels; this is also not a medical book or a chemistry book. This is a supernatural revelatory book in which I share understanding and findings from the Word of God, as well as common knowledge from medical sources, chemistry sources, metallurgy, and mineralogy sources. This information can be found anywhere; you do not need a degree to research this on your own. This revelation should increase your faith that our God created the universe—a perfect, natural realm manifest into existence by His spoken word. Because of sinful man, it is now a marred version of His heavenly expectation. Our earth is redeemed by Jesus' death, burial, resurrection, and ascension, and it reveals heavenly truth. I do not profess to be an expert in any area, only that God has revealed information to me experientially and in the scriptures. Through these resources He has shown me the spiritual and natural perspectives of angels. Carefully pray on this information yourself and seek the Holy Spirit for truth. Now, I believe you are ready to learn more!

ARCHANGELS

The first fire angels in the hierarchy are archangels. Archangels have leadership over legions of angels including seraphim, cherubim, and guardian angels. The two main archangels from scripture are Michael and Gabriel. Michael's name in Hebrew means "who is like God?" You can read about him in the endtimes, executing judgment and fighting against satan, the dragon:

> *Then war broke out in heaven. Michael and his angels fought against the dragon, and the dragon and his angels fought back. But he was not strong enough, and they lost their place in heaven. The great dragon was hurled down—that ancient serpent called the devil, or Satan, who leads the whole world astray. He was hurled to the earth, and his angels with him* (Revelation 12:7-9).

He is also revealed when Daniel had a great vision and he fasted and prayed for understanding. God dispatched the archangel Michael and it took 21 days for the answer to come.

> *Then he continued, "Do not be afraid, Daniel. Since the first day that you set your mind to gain understanding and to humble yourself before your God, your words were heard, and I have come in response to them. But the prince of the Persian kingdom resisted me twenty-one days. Then Michael, one of the chief princes, came to help me, because I was detained there with the king of Persia. Now I have come to explain to you what will happen to your people in the future, for the vision concerns a time yet to come"* (Daniel 10:12-14).

The endtimes are clarified to Daniel in the vision:

At that time Michael, the great prince who protects your people, will arise. There will be a time of distress such as has not happened from the beginning of nations until then. But at that time your people—everyone whose name is found written in the book—will be delivered (Daniel 12:1).

In Jude 1:8-9, Jude shares about ungodly people and uses the archangel Michael as a reference:

In the very same way, on the strength of their dreams these ungodly people pollute their own bodies, reject authority and heap abuse on celestial beings. But even the archangel Michael, when he was disputing with the devil about the body of Moses, did not himself dare to condemn him for slander but said, "The Lord rebuke you!"

One of the main characteristics of the archangel Michael is that he is a warfare angel. He is like God in that he shuns evil and protects the people.

Then we have Gabriel, whose name means "strength or might." He is the one who spoke to Zechariah and Mary, telling them of the children that would be born to them. He is a bearer of good news. Gabriel spoke to Zechariah:

The angel said to him, "I am Gabriel. I stand in the presence of God, and I have been sent to speak to you and to tell you this good news" (Luke 1:19).

Gabriel spoke to Mary:

In the sixth month of Elizabeth's pregnancy, God sent the angel Gabriel to Nazareth, a town in Galilee, to a virgin pledged to be married to a man named Joseph, a descendant of David. The virgin's name was Mary. The angel went to her and said, "Greetings, you who are highly favored! The Lord is with you" (Luke 1:26-28).

The last known archangel is Raphael. He is not present in the Bible but only in the book of Tobit and other books of the Apocrypha. These books are not considered the inspired Word of God. It is said in those books that Raphael was the angel present in the pool of Bethesda, which John mentions without naming the angel:

Some time later, Jesus went up to Jerusalem for one of the Jewish festivals. Now there is in Jerusalem near the Sheep Gate a pool, which in Aramaic is called Bethesda and which is surrounded by five covered colonnades. Here a great number of disabled people used to lie—the blind, the lame, the paralyzed. One who was there had been an invalid for thirty-eight years. When Jesus saw him lying there and learned that he had been in this condition for a long time, he asked him, "Do you want to get well?" "Sir," the invalid replied, "I have no one to help me into the pool when the water is stirred. While I am trying to get in, someone else goes down ahead of me." Then Jesus said to him, "Get up! Pick up your mat and walk." At once the man was cured; he picked up his mat and walked (John 5:1-9).

SERAPHIM

The angels next in the hierarchy after archangels are the seraphim. They are angels of fire that have blue or super-bright white flames. That word *seraphim* in the Hebrew is *saraph,* a burning, poisonous, fiery serpent. They actually have copper properties within them. Copper makes a blue flame.

Blue fire angels burn hotter than yellow, orange, or red seraphim or cherubim ones. When I see glory oil angels, they are blue-white or silver—they have the blue fire of the seraphim along with red and green hues to make white. They carry extreme heat. They emit the glory of the Lord. When I see the blue fire angels, I know glory flame is there.

Seraphim are distinguished by their color and their power. Their power comes from the role they play around the throne of God. When angels of fire are present, healing and purification have come. Any fire angel has healing and purification power because that is the nature of an angel, but some have more than others. It depends how close they are to the throne of God.

The properties of an angel, what they are made of, is from compounds or mineral that can withstand excessive heat. Different colors in flames can mean that certain flames are hotter than others. Blue flame is the hottest flame, whereas orange flames are not as hot. The center of a candle flame is blue and the outside is yellow and orange. We know from the Hebrew word *saraph,* associated with seraphim, that they have copper so they are blue in color, but that does not mean they do not have other flames associated with them. It just means copper is more evident. I will explain more as we go along.

ANGEL COLORS

Visible light comes in many different colors—all the colors of the rainbow. White light combines all the colors, which is why angels that are seen as white in the Word of God have all three main color groups within them—red, green, and blue. When atoms are heated to different temperatures, they produce energy at different wavelengths, resulting in different colors of light. You can see this in the flame of a candle. Some flames get hot enough that they are blue in the very center, where it is about 1400° Celsius. The next hottest flame is yellow, then orange, and finally red. Red fire is only about 800° Celsius.

Colors can also be created by burning different minerals and metals. Each element creates its own color. For example, copper produces a blue flame, lithium and strontium a red flame, calcium an orange flame, sodium a yellow flame, and barium a green flame. So when we look at the Hebrew word *saraph* and how it relates to copper, we can see that blue fire angels have copper as part of their spiritual makeup and are closer to the wick and flame of God and they carry a more intense glory fire. They burn hotter and produce a fire that is deeper and stronger than seraphim or cherubim that are yellow or orange. Blue fire angels' purpose is purification in healing.

Copper is a chemical element that helps to build our immune system. It is necessary for healthy bones, nerves, and blood vessels. It is naturally occurring everywhere in our world. We don't produce copper in our bodies; we must get it from our diet. A copper deficiency can cause fatigue, heart disease, diminished immunity, pale skin, and premature gray hair. Other symptoms can be fatigue, low energy, anemia, and low white blood cells for fighting infection.

PURIFICATION AND HEALING

I find it interesting that blue fire angels or seraphim are leaders in healing in God's kingdom. Seraphim or blue fire angels carry copper, which is good for the immune system and can combat enemy forces that try to kill the immune system. When people need a healing for copper deficiency, these are the angels that would be best equipped to bring healing to those areas. Where demonic spirits of infirmity unleashed by the enemy would come to kill, steal, and destroy someone's immune system, these angels of fire, along with Holy Spirit, do the work of healing the immune system and these particular weak areas.

In the Bible, seraphim carried coal to purify Isaiah (see Isa. 6:2,6). Coal is necessary for heat to come forth. One of the secondary elements in coal is sulfur. Copper mixed with sulfur creates copper sulfate, which can kill algae and fungus. Though copper sulfate can be dangerous in large quantities, algae and fungi are harmful impurities that copper sulfate can help expel. So imagine seraphim, angels who have copper, carrying coal, which has sulfur, from the altar of heaven. In this picture, seraphim come and purify and bring forth healing to those with deficiencies in this area.

It is true in healing ministry that when someone confesses their sin, they are confessing impurities that will release demonic strongholds. When the Holy Spirit of God touches a person and they begin to repent, they can be freed from demonic strongholds and receive healing in their bodies. The same is true when God commands seraphim to come and perform a healing on someone—it will be done with purification at the core. The heat of God and His Holy Spirit will come to convict and bring love to the core of the person, and they will be ready to ask for forgiveness and positioned to be released from the demonic stronghold and now heal their bodies. This is why repentance is so important for healing. When one confesses sin, a purification of the soul takes place. This is a normal first step for those conducting healing ministry.

This is the power of repentance and purification for healing. Seraphim located at the throne of God are purified creatures. Because of that purity, they can handle coals of fire from the pure altar of God to bring healing. They also specialize in immune, bone, and heart disorders as stated above, but they are not held back from healing in other areas too.

YELLOW, ORANGE, AND RED FIRE ANGELS

Seraphim and cherubim angels of fire that give off a yellow or orange color carry different properties. The ones with a yellow flame carry sodium, an orange flame carry calcium, and a red flame carry lithium or strontium. The kind of fire angels they are depends on the natural mineral properties they carry for healing in the earth. If the enemy unleashes specific infirmities through mineral deficiencies in the human body—such as sodium, calcium, lithium, and strontium—the angels made of these elements can bring healing.

The yellow flame angels, which have the mineral of sodium. Sodium is found in many foods, especially in the form of sodium chloride—table salt. Although we often hear about the unhealthy effects of too much salt in our diets, our bodies need sodium for normal muscle and nerve functions and to keep body fluids in balance. Low sodium levels result in fatigue, headache, muscle cramps, nausea, and irritability.

If the yellow fire angel brings coal, or sulfur, that is sodium sulfate. Homeopathics say sodium sulfate is beneficial for the liver, pancreas, intestines, and kidneys, as well as for flus and colds. Sodium sulfacetamide, a sulfa antibiotic, is used to treat several skin problems by stopping the growth of certain bacteria on the skin—bacteria that cause acne, rosacea, and seborrheic dermatitis.

This brings us to the orange flame angels that have the mineral calcium. You have probably heard of how important calcium is for strong bones. Our bones and teeth store calcium. The body also needs calcium for almost all of its functions. People often take calcium supplements to fight a deficiency in this mineral in their bodies. One of the most common results of a calcium deficiency is osteoporosis.

When we consider a calcium angel carrying a sulfur coal from God's altar, we find calcium sulfate, as mentioned before. Homeopathic medicine uses calcium sulfate against acne, abscesses, ulcers, and wounds that have become infected, and to prevent an oncoming cold or sore throat. Also signs of calcium deficiency can be numbness in arms and legs, dizziness, brain fog, premenstrual syndrome, depression, chest pains, cataracts, or seizures. It is a purifying substance when used in very small amounts.

RED, PURPLE, AND GREEN FIRE ANGELS

Strontium is found in the red fire angel. This mineral is found in seawater and soil. In your diet you get it mainly from seafood, but you can also get small amounts of it in whole milk, wheat bran, meat, poultry, and root vegetables. It may be good for bone health but its effectiveness is still being tested. I could not find in my research that strontium sulfate has any particular use in the body. However, it is like calcium in many ways, so we can assume God would use these red fire angels much the same way.

The last element is lithium, which also is present in red fire angels. It is interesting to note that lithium has been around since creation. Cosmologists believe there were originally only three elements—hydrogen, helium, and lithium. Lithium is still prevalent throughout the universe; it is all over earth, in the sea, and every organ and tissue in the human body contains lithium.

Lithium deficiencies are linked to mental health problems. Low lithium levels are seen in children with autism and persons with bipolar disorder. Some pharmaceuticals may recommend lithium to treat these disorders. A daily dose of lithium is suggested to be good for individuals with excessive mood disorders.

There are also angels of fire that can burn purple. Fireworks manufacturers make the color purple by mixing strontium and copper together. This means purple angels of fire would carry with them the healing properties of both strontium and copper. Last, the green fire angels carry barium sulfate and travel with the red and blue angels and they highlight images that are in need of healing. Barium sulfate works by coating the esophagus, stomach, or intestine with a material that is not absorbed into the body so the diseased areas can be highlighted by x-ray examination or CT scan. They can also help prepare the body for healing of digestive disorders. It is important to note that the green fire angels are associated closely with the red and blue angels and are not needed alone as they accent the work of these other angels. When you see white angels they are in a glow form of red, blue, and green together. So they are unique but carry all these properties in one. White angels make a silvery white glow, because white light contains blue, green, and red, as we said above.

HE IS LIKE A RAINBOW

The colors of the angels of fire can also be understood by relating them to the colors of the rainbow. The seven colors of the rainbow are red, orange, yellow, green, blue, indigo, and violet. Rainbows are made when sunlight enters water droplets, which bend the light and reflect it, separating it into its different wavelengths or colors.

Rainbows are very special to God. In the book of Ezekiel, the colors of the rainbow reflect the likeness and glory of the Lord:

> *Then there came a voice from above the vault over their heads as they stood with lowered wings. Above the vault over their heads was what looked like a throne of lapis lazuli, and high above on the throne was a figure like that of a man. I saw that from what appeared to be his waist up he looked like glowing metal, as if full of fire, and that from there down he looked like fire; and brilliant light surrounded him. Like the appearance of a rainbow in the clouds on a rainy day, so was the radiance around him. This was the appearance of the likeness of the glory of the Lord. When I saw it, I fell facedown, and I heard the voice of one speaking* (Ezekiel 1:25-28).

Here we see the stone lapis lazuli, which is a blue color, and then a figure of a man. The man appeared like glowing metal. The word for *voice* is the Hebrew word *kole*, which means "spark." The word for *man* is the Hebrew word *adam*. This is the second Adam, Jesus Christ. The King James Version describes Him:

> *And I saw as the colour of amber, as the appearance of fire round about within it, from the appearance of his loins even upward, and from the appearance of his loins even downward, I saw as it were the appearance of fire, and it had brightness round about.*

This color amber is the word *chashmal* in the Greek, which is bronze. The seraphim have that copper metal look also.

Then a rainbow of all the colors of fire and light showed around Him. If He has all the colors of fire and light, then the angels will also have similar colors as they are around His throne. In Revelation 4:3 we read, "And the one who sat there had the appearance of jasper and ruby. A rainbow that shone like an emerald encircled the throne."

JASPER, RUBY, AND EMERALD

Jesus' appearance on the throne is described as jasper. Jasper is the opaque form of chalcedony, usually brown, yellow, or reddish. So what is chalcedony? Chalcedony is the white, gray, or blue translucent type of quartz. This is in keeping with the color of the fire angels that look white because they have blue copper properties within them. Jasper is also considered a powerful healing stone that gives a sense of well-being.

Jesus' appearance is also described as a ruby, which you probably know is a bright red color. It is a durable, rare gem. Ruby is the red variety of the mineral corundum; all other colors of corundum aside from red are called sapphire. Rubies and sapphires are identical in all properties except for color.

Revelation 4:3 says, "A rainbow that shone like an emerald encircled the throne." Emeralds are a beryl mineral containing chromium and vanadium, which give them a brilliant green color. Chromium is a steel-gray, lustrous, hard metal that polishes very nicely and melts at a very high temperature. You may have heard it called "chrome." It is indispensable as an industrial metal because of its hardness and resistance to corrosion. Emeralds contain chromium, which means they are associated with a hard metal with a high melting point that shows as silvery white. Note this metal does not corrode; it is resistant to impurities. Likewise, around the throne of God, where it is hot with the fire of God, we have silvery white bright light being expelled. This same silvery white is what blue seraphim look like when they are shining so bright they give off a silver hue. I believe blue seraphim are a form of glory angels because of their properties and white silvery color.

The seraphim and cherubim angels of fire around His throne carry the mineral and metal properties evident with Him. This means when fire angels come in the earth realm, they are carrying the glory of God with His very own throne room properties of fire with them. This fire angel even has the same properties as the throne: "Then I saw another mighty angel coming down from heaven. He was robed in a cloud, with a rainbow above his head; his face was like the sun, and his legs were like fiery pillars" (Rev. 10:1). Again, he has a rainbow above his head, a face like the sun, and legs like fiery pillars.

THE RAINBOW COVENANT

We have all seen rainbows in the sky. They remind us of the flood that God sent to destroy the earth and the promise God made that no more floods would destroy the whole earth. To Noah He said of His covenant:

> *And God said, "This is the sign of the covenant I am making between me and you and every living creature with you, a covenant for all generations to come: I have set my rainbow in the clouds, and it will be the sign of the covenant between me and the earth. Whenever I bring clouds over the earth and the rainbow appears in the clouds, I will remember my covenant between me and you and all living creatures of every kind. Never again will the waters become a flood to destroy all life. Whenever the rainbow appears in the clouds, I will see it and remember the everlasting covenant between God and all living creatures of every kind on the earth." So God said to Noah, "This is the sign of the covenant I have established between me and all life on the earth"* (Genesis 9:12-17).

Why would God choose the rainbow as a sign of the covenant? It is because it is a sign around His throne. He is saying, "The very sign that is above My throne is the sign I am sending to the earth and its generations." This covenant between God and the earth is a pact of His love and glory. God now covers and protects the earth. I believe He sent this sign because the Messiah, Savior of the earth, would come and Jesus would die, be buried, resurrect, and ascend.

In Genesis, the rainbow was a covenant with Noah, and in the endtimes it is revealed around the throne of God in Revelation

4:3. We also see the second Adam, Jesus Messiah, with this very rainbow over His head in Ezekiel 1:28. From the beginning of the world to the end, the rainbow reveals God Himself in all His colors to us.

CHAPTER 7

SERAPHIM AND CHERUBIM

I N THE HIERARCHY OF ANGELS, SERAPHIM ARE THE NEXT HIGH-est under archangels, then cherubim and, then guardian angels. These seraphim and cherubim also carry purification and healing and also act as guards. Each angel class is similar to the others but still unique. First, we will read about the seraphim; later we will read about the purification of the cherubim.

Seraphim are referenced in Isaiah 6 as being seated above the throne of God.

> *In the year that King Uzziah died, I saw the Lord, high and exalted, seated on a throne; and the train of his robe filled the temple. Above him were seraphim, each with six wings: With two wings they covered their faces, with two they covered their feet, and with two they were flying* (Isaiah 6:1-2).

God's seraphim and cherubim live at the throne of God, so they have the greatest heat and power to command legions and tear down principalities. Seraphim fire angels give off a white or silvery blue hue because they have copper properties and they are closer to the glory of God as they are above His throne. The cherubim are around God's throne but are more categorized as being gold fire angels. Guardian angels can be yellow, orange, or red, but they are assigned to people so they are more focused on people than on the throne of God. God just designed them to be more near us than near Him. They see His face as needed, and they see cherubim and seraphim as needed. Cherubim and seraphim are the angels at the top of the hierarchy and closer to the throne giving them orders.

As you learned in prior chapters, Gabriel and Michael are fire angels that would have silvery blue flames as they are archangels and lead legions. They are at the top of the chain of command. Archangels dispatch the seraphim and cherubim angels to go and do their job.

I believe these angels will be leading the end-time revival with the archangels and will be dispatching the other fire angels around the world to bring forth the harvest. An archangel is much like an admiral in the US Navy; then blue seraphim and gold cherubim would be like captains and have charge over commanders, lieutenants commanders, lieutenants, and so on. They have charge of legions of angels, and at God's command, dispatch the orange and yellow. We see orange, yellow, and red fire angels more frequently than silvery and blue fire angels.

In this passage below, we read about the angel of Lord appearing and then the heavenly hosts with him to announce the birth of Jesus to the shepherds. This angel of the Lord would be an archangel, probably Gabriel. He would look white. The heavenly hosts would be seraphim giving off a blue-white color, cherubim of a gold hue, and guardian angels giving off an orange, yellow, or red glow. They bring joy and they have been around the angels who have been around the throne of God.

> *And there were shepherds living out in the fields nearby, keeping watch over their flocks at night. An angel of the Lord appeared to them, and the glory of the Lord shone around them, and they were terrified. But the angel said to them, "Do not be afraid. I bring you good news that will cause great joy for all the people. Today in the town of David a Savior has been born to you; he is the Messiah, the Lord. This will be a sign to you: You will find a baby wrapped in cloths and lying in a manger." Suddenly a great company of the heavenly host appeared with the angel, praising God and saying, "Glory to God in the highest heaven, and on earth peace to those on whom his favor rests"* (Luke 2:8-14).

CHERUBIM

Cherubim are angels that guard the throne. The word *cherubim* in the Hebrew means "imaginary figure." We know they guard because of their actions in certain scriptures. We know they are also above the mercy seat in the throne room and their likeness is carved on the ark of the covenant and linen curtains in the temple. They are also angels of fire and handle coal just like seraphim do. They have a golden hue or mix of orange, yellow, and red and play a vital role in Ezekiel 1–7, in the vision that Ezekiel had concerning

God's glory departing the temple after the burning of the city. In this passage, the Lord is judging Jerusalem for idolatry, and we see a lot of activity with the cherubim. These cherubim have wheels with them. They are a different variety. Ezekiel 10 says that lapis lazuli, which is a deep indigo blue color, was above the vault over the heads of the cherubim. Lapis lazuli is so blue because of the purification of mineral sulfur.

We keep seeing blue above the throne of God, above the cherubim, in stones, or in the actual blue seraphim. Ezekiel 10:1-22 shares when the Lord's glory leaves the temple, and the cherubim are part of this process.

> I looked, and I saw the likeness of a throne of lapis lazuli above the vault that was over the heads of the cherubim. The Lord said to the man clothed in linen, "Go in among the wheels beneath the cherubim. Fill your hands with burning coals from among the cherubim and scatter them over the city." And as I watched, he went in.
>
> Now the cherubim were standing on the south side of the temple when the man went in, and a cloud filled the inner court. Then the glory of the Lord rose from above the cherubim and moved to the threshold of the temple. The cloud filled the temple, and the court was full of the radiance of the glory of the Lord. The sound of the wings of the cherubim could be heard as far away as the outer court, like the voice of God Almighty when he speaks.
>
> When the Lord commanded the man in linen, "Take fire from among the wheels, from among the cherubim," the man went in and stood beside a wheel. Then one of the

cherubim reached out his hand to the fire that was among them. He took up some of it and put it into the hands of the man in linen, who took it and went out. (Under the wings of the cherubim could be seen what looked like human hands.)

I looked, and I saw beside the cherubim four wheels, one beside each of the cherubim; the wheels sparkled like topaz. As for their appearance, the four of them looked alike; each was like a wheel intersecting a wheel. As they moved, they would go in any one of the four directions the cherubim faced; the wheels did not turn about as the cherubim went. The cherubim went in whatever direction the head faced, without turning as they went. Their entire bodies, including their backs, their hands and their wings, were completely full of eyes, as were their four wheels. I heard the wheels being called "the whirling wheels." Each of the cherubim had four faces: One face was that of a cherub, the second the face of a human being, the third the face of a lion, and the fourth the face of an eagle.

Then the cherubim rose upward. These were the living creatures I had seen by the Kebar River. When the cherubim moved, the wheels beside them moved; and when the cherubim spread their wings to rise from the ground, the wheels did not leave their side. When the cherubim stood still, they also stood still; and when the cherubim rose, they rose with them, because the spirit of the living creatures was in them.

Then the glory of the Lord departed from over the threshold of the temple and stopped above the cherubim. While

I watched, the cherubim spread their wings and rose from the ground, and as they went, the wheels went with them. They stopped at the entrance of the east gate of the Lord's house, and the glory of the God of Israel was above them.

These were the living creatures I had seen beneath the God of Israel by the Kebar River, and I realized that they were cherubim. Each had four faces and four wings, and under their wings was what looked like human hands. Their faces had the same appearance as those I had seen by the Kebar River. Each one went straight ahead.

In Ezekiel 10:9, the cherubim's wheels are described as the color of topaz, which is a golden brown-yellow color. When the glory of the Lord departs, the cherubim go with the glory. Cherubim stay with the glory of the Lord; they are all around the glory. They protect His throne. They follow His command. In the sanctuary of the tabernacle, the cherubim were placed above the mercy seat.

Above the ark were the cherubim of the Glory, overshadowing the atonement cover. But we cannot discuss these things in detail now (Hebrews 9:5).

FOUR LIVING CREATURES

There are four living creatures around the throne that are somewhat like seraphim and cherubim. They are considered to be a different variety because they do not have the same appearance as the others over the throne. These creatures looked like animals and had six wings and eyes. However, they are also angels of fire because they are around the throne of God.

In the center, around the throne, were four living crea-
tures, and they were covered with eyes, in front and in
back. The first living creature was like a lion, the second
was like an ox, the third had a face like a man, the fourth
was like a flying eagle. Each of the four living creatures
had six wings and was covered with eyes all around, even
under its wings. Day and night they never stop saying:
"'Holy, holy, holy is the Lord God Almighty,' who was,
and is, and is to come." Whenever the living creatures
give glory, honor and thanks to him who sits on the throne
and who lives for ever and ever, the twenty-four elders fall
down before him who sits on the throne and worship him
who lives for ever and ever (Revelation 4:6-10).

SOUND OF CHERUBIM

Note the description of how the cherubim sound: "The sound of
the wings of the cherubim could be heard as far away as the outer
court, like the voice of God Almighty when he speaks" (Ezek.
10:5). Both the word *sound* and the word *voice* are translations of
the Hebrew word *qowl*, which means "crackling, lightness, thunder, and spark." This sound of the wings is similar to God's voice.
Think of it like the sound of a fire crackling and the wind sounds
that go with it. If you have ever listened to wood burning in a fire-
place, it has a sound like wind. This is what God's voice resembles.

The apostle John says he saw angels of fire around the throne
in a vision:

And I beheld, and I heard the voice of many angels round
about the throne and the beasts and the elders: and the

*number of them was ten thousand times ten thousand,
and thousands of thousands; saying with a loud voice,
Worthy is the Lamb that was slain to receive power, and
riches, and wisdom, and strength, and honour, and glory,
and blessing. And every creature which is in heaven, and
on the earth, and under the earth, and such as are in the
sea, and all that are in them, heard I saying, Blessing,
and honour, and glory, and power, be unto him that
sitteth upon the throne, and unto the Lamb for ever and
ever. And the four beasts said, Amen. And the four and
twenty elders fell down and worshipped him that liveth
for ever and ever* (Revelation 5:11-14 KJV).

Angels of fire surround the throne of God. They are a part of the fire of the altar. The cherubim are worshiping in this passage, singing in a loud voice. This is a different word for *voice* in the Greek; this Greek word is *phōnē*, which is rooted in the word *phainō*, which means "to lighten or shine." The root of *phainō* is *phōs*, which means "to shine or make manifest by rays, luminousness." These Greek words are also the base of the word *phēmi*, which means "to show or make known one's thoughts."

These cherubim were making known the thoughts of God, and it was coming forth as light. This was light that manifested the thoughts of God. Light has a frequency. It speaks something. By changing the frequency of light, you can change the color of the light wave.

The angels were supernaturally singing the very thoughts of God. This reminds me of Pentecost in Acts 2 when the tongues of fire came and brought forth a heavenly language—the sounds of heaven. You can read about this in Acts 2:1-3:

And suddenly there came a sound from heaven as of a rushing mighty wind, and it filled all the house where they were sitting. And there appeared unto them cloven tongues like as of fire, and it sat upon each of them. And they were all filled with the Holy Ghost, and began to speak with other tongues, as the Spirit gave them utterance.

The sound of heaven was classified as a mighty rushing wind that manifested in fire. The more I study this, the more amazed I become that the earth is simply a reflection of what is happening in heaven. If we will listen to our hearts and be mindful of God, He will reveal these amazing truths to us. The angels are carriers of the sounds and lights of heaven. They have specific minerals, metals, and properties of the throne room of God and they are the portals that bring them to us. When we come close to God, we can experience the manifestations of these phenomena by faith.

ANGELS OF FIRE BRING REVIVAL

I have many personal testimonies of my encounters with angels of fire during ministry. I shared a few before from my trip to France. They come with the glory of the Lord into meetings and they actively participate with Holy Spirit to bring fire and revival. They change atmospheres with the fire of God. They are carriers of His fire from His throne.

At another meeting I did, the fire angels came in and began to work on people's bodies, healing them right where they were out in the congregation. In this meeting, there was no laying on of hands at all. Nobody touched anybody; fire angels simply began to come.

I just said, "The Holy Spirit and fire angels are present and they will come to heal you." I could feel the angels in the atmosphere.

I do mentoring sessions with people who sign up through my website. This is a service I offer publicly to those who want to be personally counseled or mentored. They make an appointment, and I call them on the phone. They will ask for healing or revelation, and I ask God to dispatch the angels of fire to their homes while we are on the phone and they will experience the angels. One woman I ministered to this way was healed of a crippling physical disorder. She was four feet tall and could not even walk. She finished the session, went outside, and walked around her block. Her neighbor saw her walking and was surprised. She said, "God healed me."

There was another encounter I had at a women's conference in Spring, Texas. It was an amazing conference with lots of prophecy, teaching, and miracles. I had spoken on the royal table experience that I had, which is outlined in my book *Releasing Heaven*. I led everyone in a faith activation. The fire angels just came into the room while I was speaking, and it was very beautiful.

After I came down from the altar, a woman came up to me requesting prayer for healing for her friend who had cancer and had come in a wheelchair. Her faith was very high and she was ready for a healing. She told me she had never experienced this before where she saw Jesus and she could picture herself at the royal table with Him. We prayed in the spirit, and I asked the Holy Spirit and fire angels to touch her neck and spine. She began to feel the heat and the vibration and she said she wanted to get out of her chair. So we said, "Get up." We helped her stand up and barely held her arms as she began to walk. At first, her feet were kind of upside down and she was dragging the tops of her feet. Then the bottoms of her feet hit the floor, and she began to walk faster and faster with little to no help, and she began to run around the sanctuary. She said, "I am healed." The Holy Spirit, fire angels, and her increased faith from seeing Jesus at the royal table in heaven brought her a healing.

VOICE OF THE LORD AND FIRE

Fire angels are active every single day around us. They are dispatched to engage with us as a normal part of our earth realm. They are the ministering flames of fire in Hebrews 1:7: "In speaking of the angels he says, 'He makes his angels spirits, and his servants flames of fire.'" All angels are fire angels; they burn as flames of fire to bring what is needed in the earth. Flames are a commodity of heaven. Flames come from the fire of God and who He is. In Psalm 29:7, "The voice of the Lord divideth the flames of fire" (KJV).

That word for *voice* is the same one we discussed earlier—the sound of crackling, the spark, thunder, and lightness. When God speaks, it starts a spark. The angels of fire are inspired to run where He is directing or where the frequency of His voice goes. When you need healing, you first ask God. He will heal by His Holy Spirit, but He will also send the fire angels by the sound of His voice through you to come and bring healing. His voice will start a spark of revival. We are to call to God and ask him to do His work, and He will command the fire angels to move by His voice through you. When the fire angels come, that's when revival comes; that's also when healing begins to take place. Now, I want to pray for you so that you can actually have an activation to experience fire angels. You can also return to the testimony in the beginning of the book of deliverance minister Steve Hemphill, who was healed of COVID-19. I encourage you to go back and read that prayer of healing. Here are some more prayers below.

PRAYER FOR FIRE ANGELS

Lord, I praise You and I thank You right now. Father, I ask You to just bring forth Your power. Father, I just want to thank You right now that You're stirring up Your Spirit on the inside of the reader. I thank You, Father, that they're surrounded by fire angels right now. Father, I know the fire angels have been hearkening to the word that's being spoken in this book. It is Your word and Your voice starts a spark, and they are coming around. I thank You, Father, that You're beginning to heal the reader right now. Please go to that part of their body that is in pain, Father. The fire angels are beginning to touch. Healing is beginning to come right now in the name of Jesus. I thank You, Father, that spinal cord injuries are being healed. I thank You, Lord Jesus, that back and neck injuries are being healed.

I thank You, Lord, that everywhere bones and muscles are aching and hurt right now, You are sending a blue fire angel and the orange, yellow, and red ones to bring healing. Arthritis is being healed right now in the name of Jesus. I thank You, Father, that there is fire going to people's hands and to their feet right now, and

to everywhere that there may be a pain in their body.
Father, right now bring healing in their ears. Lord Jesus,
I thank You that any pain my friend is experiencing in
their knees, fire angels are coming and they are begin-
ning to touch those areas in the mighty name of Jesus.
Thank You, Father, for sending the fire angels with the
spark of Your voice.

If you feel these body areas beginning to get hot, just stay right
there and allow the fire angels to finish the work.

IMPARTATION FOR HEALING GIFTS

If you have been wanting to receive healing gifts, I want to pray an
impartation for you now.

I praise You and I thank You, Lord. I pray for my friend
to receive healing gifts right now. Father, if they have
been asking for people to be healed in their family, their
friends, their workplace, I thank You that You're begin-
ning to activate healing gifts in my friend. You are raising
up their faith, Father, so that they can step into that
place of being called by You, Lord Jesus, to be a change
agent for the kingdom so that healing would start flow-
ing through them. I thank You that You are the great
and mighty healer and that the angels are simply Your
stewards, Your servants of healing that are coming and
bringing fire. Teach us to participate with the fire angels
to bring healing to our homes and our communities. I
thank You, Father, that everywhere we speak the word
about healing, revival, and the breaking of strongholds,

Lord Jesus, these fire angels come and they do Your work, Father.

I praise You and I thank You right now that You are beginning to stir people to receive this impartation and to be able to walk in the confidence that they are surrounded by fire angels who have come to do Your bidding. Angels have come to do Your work. They are waiters on Your behalf. They're Your messengers, so we praise You and we thank You. We give You all the glory and all the honor, Father, and I thank You that my friend is being healed right now. I see people being healed of intestinal disorders and stomach disorders right now in the name of Jesus. I praise You and I thank You.

ARTHRITIS AND INFLAMMATION HEALING

Father, I ask for healing for arthritis and inflammation in the joints. I ask You, Lord, to send forth the blue, yellow and orange fire angels that carry copper sulfate, sodium sulfate and calcium sulfate to come and strengthen their joints. There are people who are receiving healing in their thighs. Lord, I see muscles that have been over-worked and stretched beyond measure. You're beginning to bring healing to them right now in the name of Jesus. I thank You for ankles and feet being healed right now. Lord, we praise You and we thank You. I see arthritis and inflammation in the hands being healed right now, Lord Jesus. We just ask You, Father, to bring that healing. After the fire angels have done what You're calling them to do, Father, I ask that there would be a coolness. Please let those areas that are aggravated begin to calm. We thank You, Father.

HEALING FOR EMOTIONAL DISORDERS

Lord, I also pray for emotional disorders right now. If people's emotions of depression, anxiety, or fear are overwhelming them, then dispatch the red fire angels to come and console the person so they would feel Your warmth, peace, and love, Father. I ask You also to dispatch the seraphim red fire angels that have lithium so they can be healed of mental and emotional pain and distress and feel Your glory, Lord Jesus. They will feel Your peace, Father, knowing that You have come to heal them emotionally as well as physically in Jesus' name. Amen.

CHAPTER 8

CHARIOTS OF FIRE

I KNOW YOU ARE EXCITED TO LEARN MORE ABOUT ANGELS OF FIRE and want to be sensitive to what's going on in your atmosphere. You want to be more aware and able to assess what God is doing so that you can meet Him there. In order to do that, we have to learn a little bit more about fire angels so that we can get the good Word in us. You know, the supernatural is amazing, but we need to also have the Word of God to be able to back up what we're saying. In Psalm 104:1-8, the Word says:

> *Praise the Lord, my soul. Lord my God, you are very great; you are clothed with splendor and majesty. The Lord wraps himself in light as with a garment; he stretches out the heavens like a tent and lays the beams of his upper chambers on their waters.* **He makes the clouds his chariot and rides on the wings of the wind.** *He makes winds his messengers,* **flames of fire his servants.** *He set the earth on its foundations; it can never be moved. You*

covered it with the watery depths as with a garment; the waters stood above the mountains. But at your rebuke the waters fled, at the sound of your thunder they took to flight; they flowed over the mountains, they went down into the valleys, to the place you assigned for them.

The Word tells us that the clouds are chariots and He rides the wings of the wind. Psalm 68:17 says, "The chariots of God are tens of thousands and thousands of thousands; the Lord has come from Sinai into his sanctuary." The chariots of God are "thousands of thousands." So who is riding them? Chariots have riders. The Lord is among them in the holy place, and the chariots of God are driven by multitudes of angels. They're representative of fire. Only a fire angel could ride a chariot of fire. Who could withstand the heat of a chariot of fire other than one who is made of the same composition?

Fire angels are a normal part of the supernatural and what God wants to do in the earth realm. He makes winds His messengers, flames of fire His servants. That word *winds* in the Hebrew is *ruach*, which is "blow or breath." This is the same word for *Spirit* we find in Genesis 1:2: "And the earth was without form, and void; and darkness was upon the face of the deep. And the Spirit of God moved upon the face of the waters" (KJV). Angels or spirits come in the form of wind. The more wind there is, the greater the fire.

TRANSFERENCE OF ANOINTING

God spoke to our church, Freedom Destiny Church, and told us to invade demonic territory and set up our church in a local bar. The Lord kept encouraging us that there were more angels with us than people. He opened the eyes of the leadership to see that we had chariots and angels of fire from heaven supporting us, and they were more than we were in number and more than the demonic could send against us. We can see this happening also in Second Kings 6. The King of Aram became enraged at Elisha the prophet and sent an army to surround him:

> *When the servant of the man of God got up and went out early the next morning, an army with horses and chariots had surrounded the city. "Oh no, my lord! What shall we do?" the servant asked. Then Elisha answered his servant and said, "Don't be afraid," the prophet answered. "Those who are with us are more than those who are with them."* And **Elisha prayed, "Open his eyes, Lord, so that he may see**.*" Then the Lord opened the servant's eyes, and he looked and saw the **hills full of horses and chariots of fire** all around Elisha* (2 Kings 6:15-17).

Just as He did for Elisha's servant, God opened our eyes that we might see. I believe that God is going to open your eyes that you might see that more of the heavenly hosts are with you than those you see around you in the flesh, like your family or your friends. The forces with you are the chariots of fire and the forces of heaven just as in Elisha's case.

When we're in a natural battle, we often feel like saying, "Lord, I don't have the resources to get through this. How can I possibly be victorious and be an overcomer?" But as we can see from these scriptures, God will open our eyes that we might see, but we have to have faith. Elisha had that kind of God-faith. Elisha knew that there was a spiritual world with chariots of fire and things that he could see in the spirit realm. He wanted others to have their eyes opened so that they would be encouraged.

If you are the only one in your family or in your church who can see, ask God to open the eyes of others so that they might see the supernatural and angelic activity as well. I'm going to pray for you at the end of this chapter. If you want more understanding of how to change atmospheres with the God-kind of faith, consider getting my other book, *Releasing Heaven*, where I explain more this kind of faith we need for the miraculous.

MANTLE ASSIGNMENTS

I want to talk a little bit more about these chariots of fire. I believe that God wants us to understand the importance of angels and heavenly encounters when we receive new mantle assignments by faith. When it is time for God to give you a new mantle assignment, there will be confirmations from leaders in your life and God that next-level assignments are here. God will supernaturally reveal to others that you have been elevated, and they will sense a new fire on you. They will see angelic hosts around you and sense spiritually that God has chosen you for a purpose.

When the power of God comes upon us, we must be ready to receive the fire of heaven. When God is giving us a new mantle assignment, the angels of fire will be present. They will be sent forth to bring us into a new revelation of this mantle God is bringing. As I shared with you earlier, whenever I was going to next levels of promotion, there was an angel that God assigned to me or something supernatural to bring forth fire and purification. In new mantle assignments, consecration is common. This means heaven is present and fire angels are present to purify you for the mantle according to the mandate sent by the throne of God. God dispatches His seraphim and cherubim to do the purification.

We can read about a dramatic encounter in Second Kings 2 where Elisha asked Elijah for a double portion of his spirit and received it, and the angels of fire were present. This story was indeed a dramatic display of a new mantle on Elisha life.

> *When they had crossed, Elijah said to Elisha, "Tell me, what can I do for you before I am taken from you?" "Let me inherit a double portion of your spirit," Elisha replied. "You have asked a difficult thing," Elijah said, "yet if you see me when I am taken from you, it will be yours— otherwise, it will not." As they were walking along and talking together, suddenly a chariot of fire and horses of fire appeared and separated the two of them, and Elijah went up to heaven in a whirlwind. Elisha saw this and cried out, "My father! My father! The chariots and horsemen of Israel!" And Elisha saw him no more. Then he took hold of his garment and tore it in two. Elisha then picked up Elijah's cloak that had fallen from him and went back and stood on the bank of the Jordan. He took the cloak that had fallen from Elijah and struck the water with it. "Where now is the Lord, the God of Elijah?" he asked. When he struck the water, it divided to the right and to the left, and he crossed over. The company of the prophets from Jericho, who were watching, said, "The spirit of Elijah is resting on Elisha." And they went to meet him and bowed to the ground before him (2 Kings 2:9-15).*

Now, why is this important? Here we have Elisha, who is Elijah's servant, asking for more of the Spirit of God. He wants a double portion. That's pretty intense. Sometimes when God opens up our eyes to the heavenlies, He's revealing to us that we are receiving a greater portion of His Spirit. We are beginning to grab hold of this spiritual world and the spiritual things, the heavenly places that He's so much a part of, and He is inviting us into that supernatural world to know Him better and to share who He is with others.

When Elisha saw Elijah leaving and going to heaven, the mantle came upon him. His eyes were open to more of heaven, so the mantle was revealed to him. If you want to go to next levels of promotion and you are asking God for this, look out, because the heavens are about to open. You cannot go to next levels without more faith and more encounters. You must be purified to encounter more of God and then be ready to share that with others. Your mantle assignment is for kingdom expansion, not so you can be promoted. Though that is nice, God is doing this amazing promotion because it is good for Him.

You must keep your eyes open to heaven as God takes you to next-level mantle assignments. Elijah made that clear to Elisha when he told him that he needed to witness Elijah being taken from him. In scripture, chariots of fire driven by fire angels reveal that fire from heaven is a very normal thing. It is a commodity that exists in the heavenly places, and it comes to earth to accomplish the purposes for which God sent it. When God brings things from heaven to earth, angels are key participators in that process.

THE FOUR CHARIOTS

As we talk about the endtimes, we must discuss the vision Zechariah had of the four chariots. He had an angel encounter and had a conversation about the various chariots and horses that were actually four spirits coming from the presence of the Lord. These chariots and horses, having been in the presence of the Lord, were around fire. These angels were swiftly carrying out judgment on the world prior to the coming of the messianic kingdom. This is a vision before our King of kings and Lord of lords shows up:

> *I looked up again, and there before me were four chariots coming out from between two mountains—mountains of bronze. The first chariot had red horses, the second black, the third white, and the fourth dappled—all of them powerful. I asked the angel who was speaking to me, "What are these, my lord?" The angel answered me, "These are the four spirits of heaven, going out from standing in the presence of the Lord of the whole world"* (Zechariah 6:1-5).

When we talk about fire angels being activated on the earth realm, what we're seeing is the heavens coming to earth. Heavenly things are happening in the natural realm, where eyes are being opened to heavenly influence and amazing miracles are happening on the earth. Advancements for end-time revival include encounters in visions with chariots, horses, and fire angels. In the end-time revival, fire will be prevalent and so will angels of fire before the coming of the Lord Jesus to rule and reign.

PRAYER OF ACTIVATION

Now I want to pray for you to have an activation, to see in the spirit, just as Elijah prayed for Elisha to have his eyes opened. This is so that you might see the angelic and who is fighting on your behalf. I believe that you will receive the impartation and be able to say just as Elisha did, "Those who are with us are more than those who are with them." We know that he got the double portion and we know that his eyes were open and he saw the chariots. I'm going to pray that you would receive that same impartation.

> We just praise You. We thank You, Lord. I ask You to open up the eyes of the reader, Father. As Elijah prayed for his servant, I'm praying, Lord, for those who are reading, that they might see that there are more in the spirit realm than what they're surrounded with. When my friends are in battles—in their homes, in their workplaces, in their communities—Lord Jesus, more are fighting with them and fighting for them than they see in the natural realm. You are sending legions of angels and chariots of fire to come and to fight the battle, to stand with those who are in need so that they might see the heavenlies and angels of fire and know they are promoted to carry new mantle assignments.

PRAYER FOR SUPERNATURAL

> Father, I thank You that the angels hearken unto the voice of the Lord. Lord, when You command, and when humans who are in the battle begin to speak the Word, You dispatch the angels. You send the fire angels. Lord,

the fire angels come to bring the revival, the strength, the power, the healing, whenever there is a need to fight the battle at that level. I thank You that You have multiple chariots of fire and armies of angels that are being dispatched to take care of me, my family, and my friends. Father, in the name of Jesus open up their eyes that they may have supernatural sight to see dreams and visions. That they may see their guardian angels and other angels working on their behalf to bring them into the kingdom, and the plans and purposes that God has for them. I praise You and I thank You right now, Lord, for eyes to be opened in Jesus' name.

CHAPTER 9

FIRE ANGELS OF PURIFICATION

L ET ME EXPLAIN WHY FIRE ANGELS ARE SO IMPORTANT AND HOW they're really relevant. The fire of God is a part of the Word of God. The fire of God comes upon our lives for purification, sanctification, consecration, healing, revival, and deliverance. When the Word of God is spoken, as we learned, a spark from God's voice starts and the fire begins. This is the power of the spoken Word of God.

CONSECRATION

Now I want to talk with you and pray with you about consecration. Fire angels are very important for commissioning and consecration. In order to be sent, we must be purified with coals from heaven. In Isaiah 6:1-10, the prophet Isaiah is talking about his commissioning by God as a prophet. Angels are communicating with one another in this passage. They are in the temple and in the throne room with God:

> *In the year that King Uzziah died, I saw the Lord, high and exalted, seated on a throne; and the train of his robe filled the temple. Above him were seraphim, each with six wings: With two wings they covered their faces, with two they covered their feet, and with two they were flying. And they were calling to one another: "Holy, holy, holy is the Lord Almighty; the whole earth is full of his glory." At the sound of their voices the doorposts and thresholds shook and the temple was filled with smoke* (Isaiah 6:1-4).

Isaiah was in a place filled with the fire of God, and the seraphim were there. This temple was hot with the fire of God. When God releases those angels and tells them to come to earth on our behalf, they've been in His presence. They carry a part of who He is and they carry His power so much that they are able to shake the earth and the temple and in their presence smoke came.

> *"Woe to me!" I cried. "I am ruined! For I am a man of unclean lips, and I live among a people of unclean lips, and my eyes have seen the King, the Lord Almighty." Then one of the seraphim flew to me with a live coal in his hand, which he had taken with tongs from the altar. With it he touched my mouth and said, "See, this has touched your lips; your guilt is taken away and your sin atoned for." Then I heard the voice of the Lord saying, "Whom shall I send? And who will go for us?" And I said, "Here am I. Send me!"* (Isaiah 6:5-8)

In this passage, we have the Father, Son, and Holy Spirit—the fire of God. The angels are around the fire of God. One is sent by God as a representative to Isaiah on the earth. A blue seraph, which is a fire angel, touched Isaiah on his mouth with a live coal. Now that's consecration. That's purification right there. God is setting up Isaiah for a commissioning. He's going to now be a sent one.

Father God sent an angel to Isaiah with a burning coal from the altar. Then Isaiah cried out, "Send me." So you see how that works—characteristics are handed down from God Himself and His throne, they are transferred to angels, then transferred to us. So we see that purification is necessary for commissioning.

Isaiah receives the burning coal from the altar of heaven. The angels bring it forth. Let's talk about this coal. This word for *coal* is the word *ritspah,* the root of which is *resheph*—a live coal, lightning, as an arrow flashing through the air, a fever, a spark. Remember that when God speaks, His voice is like a spark. So the angel is bringing a part of who God is to Isaiah to touch Isaiah.

Isaiah was earthly, so he had to be brought to a place of heavenly fire consecration. That's a fire angel connection. Then he was set apart and commissioned for service for the work that God had called him to. Isaiah's own guilt and his sin were taken away in order to be a carrier of the Word as a sent one. To be a sent one, we must be purified just as these angels are purified. We must have properties from heaven on us. We must be touched by heaven.

When Isaiah was purified with the coal, it was in the hand of the blue seraph. As we explored before, coal is comprised partly of sulfur, a purifying agent. This coal came from the holy altar of God—this was the purity of God being released. God's purity exists on the altar, and the angel and the coal are related to those properties. This means the coal that purified came from a pure vessel with some of the same properties in the angel.

It is interesting that Isaiah's skin was touched with the third most abundant element in our own body that also is used against aggravating skin disorders. The disorders of our skin can be cleansed with the healing properties that are present in fire angels and in the coal from the altar. Our lips are also skin, and when purified they will then bring forth the Word of God and carry it to places that need to be purified. The spark of the voice of the Lord in His Word will be used to continually spark our earth realm when it comes through a pure vessel, which means you must be purified to be a sent one.

You might ask, "Why is this same sulfur in both the lake of fire and in the coals that burn Isaiah's lips?" If you have smelled sulfur, it smells awful. It smells like death, actually. Why would God touch us with an element like that? The reason is because God is pure and holy and anything unholy must be touched and consecrated. His fire angels have that property. He will bring that property to earth to destroy sin.

THE NEED FOR REPENTANCE

From a spiritually purifying standpoint, coal can strengthen those who have a repentant heart and want to be healed, who know they need consecration, and who want to submit to consecration of their heart in order to prosper. However, sulfur will not work the same on an unrepentant heart. In fact, the fire of God can cause damage to those who are unrepentant. Sodom and Gomorrah would not change and sought no repentance, so the Lord used a purifying agent and rained it down from heaven.

> *By the time Lot reached Zoar, the sun had risen over the land. Then the Lord rained down* **burning sulfur** *on Sodom and Gomorrah—from the Lord out of the heavens. Thus he overthrew those cities and the entire plain, destroying all those living in the cities—and also the vegetation in the land* (Genesis 19:23-25).

This is just like the lake of fire in Revelation, which is a place for the devil and those who do not repent. It also has sulfur, which kills evil.

> *They, too, will drink the wine of God's fury, which has been poured full strength into the cup of his wrath. They will be tormented with* **burning sulfur** *in the presence of the holy angels and of the Lamb* (Revelation 14:10).
>
> *But the beast was captured, and with it the false prophet who had performed the signs on its behalf. With these signs he had deluded those who had received the mark of the beast and worshiped its image. The two of them were thrown alive into the fiery lake of* **burning sulfur** (Revelation 19:20).

This means that when God returns, He will bring with Him the fire of the altar, the burning sulfur to purify, just as the seraph with the blue flame carried the coal from heaven's altar to purify Isaiah. This shows that purification is extremely important to God. When He is about to use something or someone for His purpose it must be purified, and the coals of heaven have sulfur properties that will do this. The angels have these same sulfur properties that emit what is needed to purify in the earth realm.

Now, why is this important? Because the fire from this altar in heaven is so full of purification that God will bring it in the end-times. Those who have repentant hearts can handle the coals of heaven, which will make them new and consecrate them for future use in the kingdom. If you have a repentant heart, you can handle the purification that is coming from heaven to set you apart for kingdom work in the endtimes as part of the army of God. If you are unrepentant, this same fire will destroy you instead.

Now is the time to repent and ask God for forgiveness! God knows you want to be set apart and consecrated, made holy as He is holy, so just talk to him and confess your mistakes, sin, worry, and fears and He will cleanse you, circumcise your heart, and send you spiritual angels to purify you in the name of Jesus. The curse of sin, condemnation, and guilt went on the cross of Jesus, so all you must do now is simply ask and it shall be done and you are saved, healed, and redeemed. God will make you mighty now for Him!

After the coal touched his lips, God gave Isaiah his new commission—to call God's people to open their eyes and ears and hearts and turn to Him and be healed. You must be consecrated in order for your commissioning to take place. If you want to be sent out—sent to nations, sent to churches, sent on the streets to evangelize—you need to be commissioned to do that. God will send a fire angel to commission you. You are going to be put in a place where you are purified, sanctified, consecrated, and set apart. Then you'll find that your spirit begins to cry out, "Lord, send me!" That was Isaiah's response.

When you know your heart is clean, it is a supernatural thing. You can pray and fast and ask God to commission you for service. He wants to. It's your time and season!

PRAYER OF PURIFICATION

I just want to pray for you right now:

Lord, I know that there are people reading this and their hearts are either leaping for joy as they are ready or they feel like they are so far from ready and are almost fearful. Lord, I know You want to commission them for service in the kingdom. I thank You, God, that You will look at each heart individually and will begin to speak. Lord, cause the reader now to rest in Your Spirit as You speak Your heart to them.

Take some time to rest, and maybe you want to even come back to this chapter later after praying and fasting, when you know you are ready. God wants to commission you!

We praise You, Lord, for loving us and sending Jesus so we can be cleansed by the blood of the Lamb. When we seek Your heart and face we become like You and we can easily confess our hearts to You. Make us pure and holy like You and send us out to do Your work in the kingdom. We love You!

I thank You that You are sending fire angels from heaven now. Lord, the reader has set themselves apart through fasting, praying, and giving. They have cried out to You. They have asked You, Father, for certain things in regard to the kingdom of God and You are calling them to be

155

set apart right now. I thank You that You are sending an
angel, Father, that is going to touch them in their spirit.

You're being touched right now in Jesus' name, right in your
spirit, right on your lips. Your mouth now is being consecrated and
you are going to speak the oracles of God. Your spirit is being baptized by fire and fire is beginning to come forth from your mouth.
You're going to speak in a heavenly language and in your native
tongue—English, Spanish, whatever native language you speak.
You're going to have a voice that sparks nations. You're going to
change nations. You're going to have a voice that's going to cause
people to repent and come to know the Lord as their Savior. You're
going to have a voice that's going to bring healing. You're going
to have a voice that's going to transform people's souls and transform nations. I praise You and I thank You right now, Father,
that the reader is being commissioned by You, set apart with the
fire of God.

Your lips will start to be on fire right now; your spirit will
stir with fire right now in the mighty name of Jesus. Just begin
to break out in tongues right now in the mighty name of Jesus.
God is consecrating you. He is setting you apart. He is positioning
you right now to be the person He wants to use in the kingdom.
I praise You and I thank You, Lord, in the mighty name of Jesus!
We love You, Lord! Thank You for using us!

FLAMES IN A BUSH

We have been talking about being consecrated, set apart, purified,
and sanctified for the Lord. The fire angels are carriers of the fire
of heaven. They are carriers of the throne room of God. When the

Lord wants to come in to touch you, He sends a servant messenger, an angel. I am sure you are very familiar with the story of Moses and the burning bush.

> *Now Moses kept the flock of Jethro his father in law, the priest of Midian: and he led the flock to the backside of the desert, and came to the mountain of God, even to Horeb. And the angel of the Lord appeared unto him in a flame of fire out of the midst of a bush: and he looked, and, behold, the bush burned with fire, and the bush was not consumed. And Moses said, I will now turn aside, and see this great sight, why the bush is not burnt. And when the Lord saw that he turned aside to see, God called unto him out of the midst of the bush, and said, Moses, Moses. And he said, Here am I. And he said, Draw not nigh hither: put off thy shoes from off thy feet, for the place whereon thou standest is holy ground* (Exodus 3:1-5 KJV).

The bush was on fire, but it didn't burn up. Now what's happening here is consecration is beginning. Moses sees the bush and he's called over to it because it's a bush that's not burning up, and God speaks to him. And Moses says, "Here I am." God says, "Listen, don't come any closer. I want you to take off your sandals." This is an act of bowing down to the Lord, recognizing the fire of God is part of consecration and sanctification, a setting apart. What is so important here is that the Lord Himself, YHWH, was present in the flame. We know fire is a characteristic of God and His holiness and purity, and we know that where He is, fire angels are present. We already established that the seraphim and cherubim are above His throne. They are where He is and they carry the same fire properties that He does.

I believe at this time on the mountain, angels were there because God was there in the flame and the fire of God. The scripture says the Lord is present, but where the Lord is present so are the angels of the Lord. Here again we see an angel of the Lord and proper positioning for purification and sanctification in holiness.

Fire angels are present during sanctification and consecration. Here, Moses is positioned to go and do his kingdom duty just as Isaiah was positioned in his commissioning to do his kingdom duty. After purification, we find Moses getting ready to go forth in his commissioning.

ELIJAH FIRE ENCOUNTER

Where the fire of God is, the angels of fire are present to assist and help. They are around the altar and are dispatched from there. As you read about the power of fire angels, keep in mind this scripture:

The Lord has established his throne in heaven, and his kingdom rules over all. Praise the Lord, you his angels, you mighty ones who do his bidding, who obey his word. Praise the Lord, all his heavenly hosts, you his servants who do his will. Praise the Lord, all his works everywhere in his dominion (Psalm 103:19-22).

Elijah was one who carried the anointing and mantle of God to bring forth fire from heaven. In First Kings 18, we see the fire of God coming from the altar of heaven to the earth realm. Here Elijah is in the showdown on Mount Carmel with the impure prophets of Baal, the false god. We see in this encounter that fire is the tool God used in order to reveal Himself and show His purity and holiness. He brings fire to bring forth the overcoming and the victory at Mount Carmel.

King Ahab and Queen Jezebel were classified as ones who had "abandoned the Lord's commands and have followed the Baals" (1 Kings 18:18). The Baals were false gods. This was an abomination to God, and He was not going to put up with it any longer. He wanted to show Himself through the prophet Elijah to the idolaters of this day. Elijah and the prophets of Baal each built an altar and prayed for fire to fall on their offering. Elijah built his altar out of twelve stones, representing the tribes of Israel, to show that God was the God of Israel and He was in charge.

The false prophets were unsuccessful in their fervent prayers to Baal. When it came to Elijah's turn, he had them pour buckets and buckets of water over his altar until it was soaked. Finally, he prayed:

> *At the time of sacrifice, the prophet Elijah stepped forward and prayed: "Lord, the God of Abraham, Isaac and Israel, let it be known today that you are God in Israel and that I am your servant and have done all these things at your command. Answer me, Lord, answer me, so these people will know that you, Lord, are God, and that you are turning their hearts back again." Then the fire of the Lord fell and burned up the sacrifice, the wood, the stones and the soil, and also licked up the water in the trench. When all the people saw this, they fell prostrate and cried, "The Lord—he is God! The Lord—he is God!"* (1 Kings 18:36-39)

Now the amazing thing is God answered Elijah by fire. That was the language of heaven. Remember, God's voice sets up a spark. When God speaks it starts a spark and the angels of fire are inspired to run to where He is directing or where the frequency of His voice goes. So when God hears us and answers our cry, it is like a spark from heaven that starts a forest fire, and we can feel it in our spirit, soul, and body and know He has answered. God answers with His purification fire, and the angels are above His throne and they are with Him when He does this. We can know from the position of the seraphim and cherubim near Him that He would dispatch them to assist Elijah. He would pour down the fire from His altar and have the fire angels around it carry the purifying fire of God to this Mount Carmel showdown, killing the impure Baal gods and prophets. Anytime God shows up where there is evil present, He brings His purifying fire as that is a characteristic of Him.

So what exactly is happening here? The fire of God is revealing God Himself and His purity. He is turning the hearts back to Him because they see His fire. That is what First Kings 18:37 says: "Answer me, Lord, answer me, so these people will know that you, Lord, are God, and that you are turning their hearts back again."

The fire of God purifies people's hearts and holiness begins to reign so they can be set back on a course of alignment. This fire will align us with God and set us up for revival. Where hearts of people turn back, revival comes as people's hearts return home to Him.

YOUR FIRE ENCOUNTER

When the fire of God comes, there are miracles and there are healings, turning people's hearts back to Him. People get out of wheelchairs. The blind see, the deaf hear, and the fire angels touch every part of our bodies. They bring the healing, the restoration, all of that in conjunction with the power of the Holy Spirit. It's the Holy Spirit and the fire angels together.

> *Then the fire of the Lord fell and burned up the sacrifice, the wood, the stones and the soil, and also licked up the water in the trench. When all the people saw this, they fell prostrate and cried, "The Lord—he is God! The Lord— he is God!"* (1 Kings 18:38-39)

When Elijah called for the fire, angels of fire were present and they brought down fire from heaven. God didn't leave his throne room for that. He just sent the fire. He sent angels with the fire to come down and start this process. The heavenly hosts were watching as God was being glorified. God was being worshiped as the one true living God over Baal. Elijah spoke the word and the fire showed up!

Wherever the fire of God is made manifest, the angels are a conduit for that. They are part of the process, servants of the Lord. They would have been there to be a part of it and watch it and participate.

TOUCHED BY FIRE

*When Jesus came down from the mountainside, large crowds followed him. A man with leprosy came and knelt before him and said, "Lord, if you are willing, you can make me clean." Jesus reached out his hand and **touched** the man. "I am willing," he said. "Be clean!" Immediately he was cleansed of his leprosy* (Matthew 8:1-3).

This word for *touched* is the Greek word *haptomai*, the reflexive form of the verb *hapto*, which means "to fasten to, to adhere to" and "to fasten fire to a thing, kindle, light, set on fire." This word also appears with the woman with the issue of blood:

> *Just then a woman who had been subject to bleeding for twelve years came up behind him and* **touched** *the edge of his cloak. She said to herself, "If I only* **touch** *his cloak, I will be healed." Jesus turned and saw her. "Take heart, daughter," he said, "your faith has healed you." And the woman was healed at that moment* (Matthew 9:20-22).

A fire had to be set in order for the healing to come forth. When Jesus did His miracles, the presence of God was there with fire, and the fire angels were present. Where God is, the angels are present. When healings take place, they are present, as they assist in the purification and healing process. When fire comes, it is there to bring healing, consecration, sanctification, and purification. Fire consumes things. It makes things new. It reveals God's authority. Fire is necessary for us to be in revival. In revival, when people are receiving the baptism of the Holy Spirit, there are fire angels present.

It's also why healings take place in the glory of God—because God's consecrated servants are there in the celebration, doing what God has called them to do. They are calling God's fire to the meetings where we see the healing, the restoration, and the wholeness. These angels also come to help burn people's souls with love and passion for God. They burn off disorders and things that are impure and do not need to be there. When impurity is burned off, then a new passion and commitment for God comes.

I believe that your faith has been increased through better understanding how these messengers of God operate. When the Lord wants to bring revival and healing and restoration and consecration, He uses fire angels in order to do His work. Let us just enter now into a place of prayer for a fire impartation.

FIRE IMPARTATION

We just thank You so much, Lord, for all that we have learned about these fire angels. I ask You, Father, to bring the reader, in their heart and in their mind, to that place of availability and openness, Lord, to receive the word, to hear it, to grow in it, to build their faith in the area of understanding the fire of God and these messengers that You send forth. I thank You, Father, for manifesting the miraculous, for sightings of fire angels in the natural and in the spiritual, and for miraculous connection with Your fire realms. Lord Jesus, it is so thrilling to be close to You and burn with that level of passion and understanding and growth. Just to see You use Your people in their purpose, destiny, and in the area of healing. It is amazing to see how You use fire to heal those who are in need, Father. Lord, I give You glory, honor, praise, and thanksgiving, because I know You are removing the veil off the eyes of those who are reading this book. They're going to have dreams and visions and see into the spirit realm and learn and grow in this area.

Father, we give You glory, honor, praise, and thanksgiving for our angels of fire. We thank You that they do Your bidding. We thank You that they're messengers of Yours, Father, that sit in the throne room and know and understand the characteristics and the nature of God. We praise You and thank You, Father, that we are on the receiving end of that. Help us, Lord Jesus, to better understand who You are and the created beings that You've sent forth in the angels. We seek Your face. We worship You only. We do not worship angels. We pray to You only, Father, and we give You glory, honor, praise, and thanksgiving. Thank You, Jesus, for Your death, burial, resurrection, and ascension that positions us to be seated with You in heavenly places. This position means we have our eyes opened from heavenly places to be able to receive all that You want to give us, Father.

We thank You, Lord Jesus, for the guardian angels that You have sent to us to help us fulfill the assignments that You've given us on the earth. We thank You for equipping us to work and participate together with angels of fire for the kingdom of God. We ask for more supernatural encounters as they share with us who You are and give us understanding about the heavenly place You are calling us to live from in these heavenly times. Our sight, hearing, smell, taste, and touch are open to keep learning in the spirit realms until we are fully seated with You, not only in spirit and soul but in body too. Give us wisdom in these endtimes as Your church that has the power and authority of the King on the earth. Let us stand for righteousness, peace, and justice as You do. We love You. Amen!

CHAPTER 10

ASCENSION ANGELS

W HAT IS AN ASCENSION ANGEL AND HOW IS THIS PERTINENT to the ministry of angels in the end-time revival? Before I teach on this, you must first understand the differences between the resurrection life and ascension life. The resurrection life is a life of walking in the power of the Lord that overcomes sin, death, and the grave. This is the beginning of our walk with Christ. He died on a cross for our sins and was buried and resurrected so that we might have eternal life. However, eternity starts today and you are now carrying eternity in your body on the earth. Jesus was eternity walking on the earth. He was with the Father and Holy Spirit before deciding to come to the earth to die for our sins. He walked in the earthly and soulish realms but maintained a heart focus on the Lord the entire time. This opened Him up to the ascension life.

The ascension life is another developmental step of faith beyond the resurrection life, and it is made possible by Jesus' ascension. The word *ascension* in the Greek is the word *anabaino,* which means to arise, ascend up, climb, go, grow, rise, spring up, and come up. This is a life on the rise! Ascension life means living daily above the earthly and soulish realms in the heavenly realms. Your body is here on earth, but your mind and heart are in the ascension realms. Overcoming sin, death, and the grave is not even your focus; you are way beyond that in a place of peace, rest, faith, and giving. The benefits of heaven are flowing through you. Angelic activity that surrounds the glory on the earth flows from this realm. Most of the church of Jesus Christ is still trying to overcome sin, death, devils, and the grave. Jesus made a way already, but they have not yet entered the understanding of the ascension life.

Now because of Jesus' death, burial, resurrection, and ascension, we have been given the benefits of fellowship with the Father, through the power of Holy Spirit, and also the place of peace and rest and the positional seat of overcoming sin, death, and the grave. This is the next dimension of living in heaven on earth. Jesus is seated in the heavenlies next to the Father. We are seated next to Him, and we now have ascension power that comes when we operate in our heavenly position in the earth realm. This is a whole way of living that gives us access to a realm that Jesus had by faith so we can prepare ourselves, others, and this world for end-time revival.

Yes, we have the Holy Spirit, the gift of God's divine presence, and this is immeasurable, but we also have access to the realms of ascension because of our position in Christ. This access brings an increase in relationship with the Father and greater confidence when walking the earth realm to bring forth the glory. We have Holy Spirit power and ascension power. You may say, "I thought I had a new position with the resurrection?" You do, but that is the power to overcome sin, death, and grave. There was more that Jesus did when He ascended that gave us power to operate in a realm of greater peace, rest, and relationship with the Father that impacts our earth realm. Yes, the resurrection increases these things too, but the ascension goes beyond this. A key verse that helps us understand the difference is John 20:11-18, in which Mary meets Jesus after His resurrection:

> *Now Mary stood outside the tomb crying. As she wept, she bent over to look into the tomb and saw two angels in white, seated where Jesus' body had been, one at the head and the other at the foot. They asked her, "Woman, why are you crying?" "They have taken my Lord away,"* *she said, "and I don't know where they have put him."* *At this, she turned around and saw Jesus standing there, but she did not realize that it was Jesus. He asked her, "Woman, why are you crying? Who is it you are looking for?" Thinking he was the gardener, she said, "Sir, if you have carried him away, tell me where you have put him, and I will get him." Jesus said to her, "Mary." She turned toward him and cried out in Aramaic, "Rabboni!" (which means "Teacher"). Jesus said, **"Do not hold on to me, for I have not yet ascended to the Father.** Go instead to my brothers and tell them, '**I am ascending to my Father and your Father, to my God and your God.**'"* *Mary Magdalene went to the disciples with the news: "I have seen the Lord!" And she told them that he had said these things to her.*

There is clearly more to understand than the resurrection. Jesus was going to the place of God's sovereign rulership that would now make a new way for us to live on the earth. Yes, there is a new way to live on the earth. This was different from overcoming the power of sin, death, and the grave; that has already happened when the resurrection occurred. If we want to see end-time revival and angelic activity, we must begin to move into freely operating in the realms of the ascension life that Jesus gave us. This is a way of operating in the glory on the earth.

COURAGEOUS HEART

The church has been stuck at the power of the resurrection, but we must get on to the ascension. Then we will see revival in the earth. The angels know this because they are with Jesus and the Father; they live in that realm and want us to live there too. For this, we must be courageous. Jesus was courageous. He was courageous to die, be buried, resurrect, and ascend so that we can now walk in the earth with no separation between us and the Father.

> *Jesus answered, "I am the way and the truth and the life. No one comes to the Father except through me. If you really know me, you will know my Father as well. From now on, you do know him and have seen him." Philip said, "Lord, show us the Father and that will be enough for us." Jesus answered: "Don't you know me, Philip, even after I have been among you such a long time? Anyone who has seen me has seen the Father. How can you say, 'Show us the Father'? Don't you believe that I am in the Father, and that the Father is in me? The words I say to you I do not speak on my own authority. Rather, it is the Father, living in me, who is doing his work. Believe me*

when I say that I am in the Father and the Father is in me; or at least believe on the evidence of the works themselves. Very truly I tell you, whoever believes in me will do the works I have been doing, and they will do even greater things than these, because I am going to the Father. And I will do whatever you ask in my name, so that the Father may be glorified in the Son. You may ask me for anything in my name, and I will do it" (John 14:6-14).

It is necessary for us to know that Jesus made a way for us to do greater works on the earth through His resurrection and ascension. We can walk in this power on the earth. We must remain connected to the Father and understand that in our heart we are that close to Him all the time. Take time before you read further to reflect on this fact so that you can be prepared to receive an impartation by faith. Be courageous in your heart because you are connected to the Father through the Holy Spirit because of what the Son Jesus did!

THADDEUS THE ASCENSION ANGEL

As you read my account with this angel Thaddeus, be encouraged—God wants to give you a courageous heart to move into the realms where you begin to be a harvester for the end-time revival. Keep in mind that this vision helps us establish the necessity of living the ascension life in the earth realm.

In the middle of the night, I was praying in my church sanctuary and I had an encounter with a huge angel named Thaddeus in a vision. This name *Thaddeus* means "courageous heart" in Greek. I saw this vision of a huge angel with a wingspan that covered the length of my church sanctuary. He came down from heaven and rested between the chairs facing the altar and the altar itself. He stood with his back to the altar. He bowed his head and kneeled as soon as he hit the ground, so I never saw his face. He rested there and above him were rays of glory light, very white, coming from a portal in the ceiling that opened to heaven. These rays were ascension rays. How do I know? Because when he landed, he was bringing heaven to earth. He was opening up a passageway. Now anyone who ministered on the altar would be in the ascension area, the heavenly place.

The Lord spoke to me in the vision and showed me that the ascension angel, Thaddeus, was revealing that ascension actually begins right here on earth. Because of the resurrection and ascension of Jesus, all we have to do is believe and we can operate in this now. Thaddeus was revealing that the divisional lines between earth and heaven are only there by unbelief. When we believe we are ministering in the ascension places, then we are—that is how thin the divide is. When the ascension came, it opened a portal for us to minister in the earth as if in heaven, just as Jesus did. He walked the earth but ministered from a heavenly perspective. He lived the ascension life while on the earth. His relationship with the Father was key for how He handled Himself in the earth realm. He did not stop seeking relationship with the Father while He walked the earth. He was 100 percent God and 100 percent man. He operated out of His body but kept His mind and heart on relationship with the Father. That is what we need to do if we want to see the ascension life happen on the earth. We have to get to the peace of a divine relationship with the Father that goes beyond fighting sin, death, and the grave.

This angel revealed that the veil has been ripped and there is no division between earth and heaven, only what we give it. When Jesus died on the cross, the veil in the Temple was torn. This shows us that there is now nothing that separates us from God. When Jesus walked the earth, nothing separated Him from relationship with His Father, but sin still separated us. Now there is no separation for us, but we still often live like there is this separation.

The Word tells us of our perfect position that we have on the earth because of the resurrection and ascension of Jesus. We are "predestined to be conformed to the image of His Son, that He might be the firstborn among many brethren" (Rom. 8:29 NKJV). This means we now have the power through the resurrection and ascension to live like Jesus did on the earth, with no separation from the Father—this is the ascension life.

> *For I am convinced that neither death nor life, neither angels nor demons, neither the present nor the future, nor any powers, neither height nor depth, nor anything else in all creation, will be able to separate us from the love of God that is in Christ Jesus our Lord* (Romans 8:38-40).

If nothing can separate us, then we should be able to walk on the earth now from this perspective. Jesus "is also risen, who is even at the right hand of God, who also makes intercession for us" (Rom. 8:34 NKJV). We are as close to Him as we can be—just as close as He is to the Father because of what He has done. This is the kind of attitude we must have in the endtimes to quicken ourselves to be participators with God for end-time revival.

> *What then shall we say to these things? If God is for us, who can be against us? He who did not spare His own*

Son, but delivered Him up for us all, how shall He not with Him also freely give us all things? Who shall bring a charge against God's elect? It is God who justifies. Who is he who condemns? It is Christ who died, and furthermore is also risen, who is even at the right hand of God, who also makes intercession for us. Who shall separate us from the love of Christ? Shall tribulation, or distress, or persecution, or famine, or nakedness, or peril, or sword? (Romans 8:31-35 NKJV)

So if nothing can separate us, why do we act like this? Because the earthly and soulish realms tell us lies that we are separate from the love of Christ and not truly unified with God. Yes, these are lies. The church must turn away from these lies if we expect to participate with the angels to usher in the end-time harvest. The veil is removed; nothing separates us from God. When we operate like this, miracles, healings, salvation, and deliverance happen because heaven has permeated the earth realm.

Now if the ministry that brought death, which was engraved in letters on stone, came with glory, so that the Israelites could not look steadily at the face of Moses because of its glory, transitory though it was, will not the ministry of the Spirit be even more glorious? If the ministry that brought condemnation was glorious, how much more glorious is the ministry that brings righteousness! For what was glorious has no glory now in comparison with the surpassing glory. And if what was transitory came with glory, how much greater is the glory of that which lasts! (2 Corinthians 3:7-11)

Moses had the glory of the Lord upon him when he received the law. The law convicts us of sin and leads us to Christ, but it is not the fulfillment—it is only a shadow of the things to come. When Christ died, was buried, and resurrected, we became positioned to have the veil removed. The glory we can experience now in our earthly bodies comes when we remember the veil is taken away and we can freely minister in the freedom of the ascension life, which is peace and rest because of what Jesus has done. The ascension says we have the glory surrounding us and deep relationship with the Father that goes beyond the law, sin, death, and the grave, but now is freedom revealing itself in the earth.

> *But whenever anyone turns to the Lord, the veil is taken away. Now the Lord is the Spirit, and where the Spirit of the Lord is, there is freedom. And we all, who with unveiled faces contemplate the Lord's glory, are being transformed into his image with ever-increasing glory, which comes from the Lord, who is the Spirit* (2 Corinthians 3:16-18).

We are being called to live in a realm of glory because the veil was taken away. We have this access now. When we allow this veil to be removed and we enter the realm of the ascension, we can now see the Lord's glory and begin to operate with Him in confidence and courage on the earth. We cannot usher in the harvest without this knowledge of ascension power because otherwise we operate earthly and we must operate heavenly. We have heavenly resources, but they only work from heavenly perspectives.

ANGELS PARTICIPATE WITH FAITH

The angels come to participate with those who have this mind-set. They want to be where the glory resides on the earth, and they will join with those who operate this way by faith. They will see you as one who lives and breathes in God, and they will come to join in. As we live by faith, we empower them for hope of the second coming of Christ. They follow our lead in this area as we speak the Word of God, and we become ones they can follow. God gave us authority and because of what Jesus did we have dominion in the earth. When we begin to act like we have the dominion Jesus bought for us, angelic hosts engage with us. Angels know the will of God, and when they see us operating in His will they join us. They are not going to join you if you are living in unbelief or inviting demonic angels to participate with unbelief and lies. If we want the power of heaven behind us, we must act worthy of it. Learning and understanding the realms of ascension living opens you up to encounters that prepare you for participation with angels in the end-time harvest.

CHAPTER 11

ANGELS OF PROTECTION

IN THIS CHAPTER WE WILL LOOK AT SCRIPTURE RELATED TO angels that protect us. Our guardian angels are assigned by God for the purpose of protection. They answer to seraphim and cherubim. They receive orders from the throne room of God. They can also carry forth fire as necessary. Here is a story of how a guardian angel protected our daughter.

ALEXANDRIA'S GUARDIAN ANGEL

It was a cold day in Scotland on New Year's Eve, December 31, 2000, and we were on a family vacation and staying in a bed and breakfast in northern Scotland. We were invited to an evening bonfire. The party was across from our farmhouse, beyond a deep ditch that was four or five feet deep. There was a small waterfall going out into the loch. I was preparing the kids to go out to the party. My husband Adam came in and asked me to send Alex out to him in a bit. But I misheard him and just sent Alex out at that moment. Adam went to do something else before getting her. It was dark, and there was no way a young child could go over that deep ditch. There was no light except for the light of the bonfire. When Adam came back to get Alexandria, he said, "OK, I'm ready for Alex."

I said, "What? I already sent her out. I thought you were out there." He said no, and we went back and forth for about 30 seconds. Then we realized, wait, where is Alex? Adam frantically went out looking for her while I stayed with the other two kids.

Adam asked the people by the bonfire and they hadn't seen her. He was trying not to freak out. When he came back and said, "I can't find her!" I was *not* calm, as any mother would not be. I had Nick and Samantha, a four-year-old and a two-year-old, but we all went outside again to look for Alex.

Then all of a sudden, there's Alex. She was just standing by Adam, all wet. Adam said, "Honey, Honey, oh my gosh, where were you? Where were you?"

She said, "This guy picked me up out of the water, in the little ditch." Adam asked who he was and she said, "I don't know." Then we asked all the people and none of them had found Alex or helped her out of the water. She was soaking wet when we got her and she said she fell in the ditch with the water, yet she acted like nothing was wrong. She did feel bad because she went by herself to the bonfire, because she thought she was big girl and could do it, but she didn't know the ditch was there. She wasn't hurt. She wasn't bruised. We have never been able to figure out who rescued her. It must've been an angel.

This angelic being appeared like a human figure. Alex did not describe this person as having wings, just that he picked her up out of the ditch and water and set her on dry land. In Hebrews 13:2, the Word says, "Be not forgetful to entertain strangers: for thereby some have entertained angels unawares" (KJV). Angels of protection are around us continually. God has assigned angels to protect us from all kinds of dangerous situations that we are unaware of. We have our guardian angels that are protectors, but there are also legions of angels who are protectors in all kinds of situations. When God wants us to come into the place He has prepared for us, He sends angels to protect us and carry us into those promised places.

LOT'S GUARDIAN ANGELS

When we think of God sending angels of protection, we cannot forget the encounter Lot had with two angels that entered Sodom, the evil city, before God destroyed it. Lot was at the city gate and he saw these two angels that looked like men come into the city. They did not have wings or appear to be a spirit body, yet Lot apparently recognized them as angels immediately.

> *The two angels arrived at Sodom in the evening, and Lot was sitting in the gateway of the city. When he saw them, he got up to meet them and bowed down with his face to the ground. "My lords," he said, "please turn aside to your servant's house. You can wash your feet and spend the night and then go on your way early in the morning." "No," they answered, "we will spend the night in the square." But he insisted so strongly that they did go with him and entered his house. He prepared a meal for them,*

baking bread without yeast, and they ate. Before they had gone to bed, all the men from every part of the city of Sodom—both young and old—surrounded the house (Genesis 19:1-4).

When men of the city came to violate the angels and Lot's family, the angels protected them:

But the men inside reached out and pulled Lot back into the house and shut the door. Then they struck the men who were at the door of the house, young and old, with blindness so that they could not find the door. The two men said to Lot, "Do you have anyone else here— sons-in-law, sons or daughters, or anyone else in the city who belongs to you? Get them out of here, because we are going to destroy this place. The outcry to the Lord against its people is so great that he has sent us to destroy it" (Genesis 19:10-13).

The angels are identified as "men." They are men who are specifically called to destroy evil and protect Lot and his family. Lot was very hesitant to leave the city, even though it was evil, but even in Lot's obstinacy the angels carried out the will of God.

The angels began the process, but the Lord ended the process by fully destroying the evil city. What this tells us is that angels are messengers sent by God and they will many times pave a way for God to come and do what only He can do.

DANIEL'S GUARDIAN ANGEL

Let us continue to learn of angels of protection and how they work with those who are considered righteous before the Lord. In the book of Daniel, the prophet Daniel, who served King Darius, had made some political enemies who desired to see Daniel lose his power and favor with the king. These deceitful, jealous men passed a decree that no one could worship any god other than the king for thirty days. This decree was aimed at trapping Daniel for his commitment and service to the Lord, but no matter the deadly agendas of others, God knows a righteous man. Daniel was not going to worship anyone but God, especially not a man, even King Darius, who was his friend. Here is Daniel's righteous reaction to the edict:

> *Now when Daniel learned that the decree had been published, he went home to his upstairs room where the windows opened toward Jerusalem. Three times a day he got down on his knees and prayed, giving thanks to his God, just as he had done before. Then these men went as a group and found Daniel praying and asking God for help* (Daniel 6:10-11).

These men were determined to expose Daniel and bring him to the king and then hold the king captive to his own law. This still happens all the time. People conjure up agendas to raise themselves up, and God comes to protect His people.

Darius was forced to throw Daniel into the lions' den, but he was rooting for Daniel and for Daniel's God to come through and rescue him:

> *So the king gave the order, and they brought Daniel and threw him into the lions' den. The king said to Daniel, "May your God, whom you serve continually, rescue you!"* (Daniel 6:16)

The king had governmental authority over the nation. When he asked that Daniel's God rescue him, we see the angelic hosts dispatched to rescue Daniel. We do not even read that Daniel asked for the angels, but this king acted in the governmental authority he carried in the nation and believed in the goodness of Daniel's God, and God released the angels. Daniel told the king:

> *My God sent his angel, and he shut the mouths of the lions. They have not hurt me, because I was found innocent in his sight. Nor have I ever done any wrong before you, Your Majesty* (Daniel 6:22).

So God sent the angel and shut the mouths of the lions because of Daniel's innocence, and also because Daniel was righteous in serving his king. I think it is interesting that the satraps and prefects ended up dying at the hands of the very law they intended to kill Daniel:

> *The king was overjoyed and gave orders to lift Daniel out of the den. And when Daniel was lifted from the den, no wound was found on him, because he had trusted in his God. At the king's command, the men who had falsely accused Daniel were brought in and thrown into the lions' den, along with their wives and children. And before they reached the floor of the den, the lions overpowered them and crushed all their bones* (Daniel 6:23-24).

In essence, these men who developed a plan to kill Daniel were lions themselves. They sought to kill Daniel with the mouth of the law. When we attempt to kill others with our tongues, the very ill we speak will come back on us and kill us.

The angelic hosts were dispatched to accomplish God's purposes and kill the evil, lying forces in the den. Once the lying spirits were eradicated, Daniel's God could rule over the land at the call of King Darius himself.

Daniel trusted God in the midst of this terrible betrayal and God prevailed. When demonic strongholds are defeated by the confession of righteous men, God is enthroned in their place. You see this in governments throughout the world. Righteous, praying men and women reveal the demonic governments; angelic help comes to the rescue to overturn the ruling evil; and then God takes His rightful place in the government as the leader proclaims God as King. Then God will bless the earthly leader with everything they need to accomplish God's purpose on the earth. Sometimes godly people seem to be persecuted for worshiping God, but God is exposing the evil in order to remove it and appoint or strengthen a godly leader so God Himself can rule in that nation.

We have seen governmental leaders in the world who were overthrown by people who refused to continue to allow those evil forces to remain. That is what wars in the earth realm are all about. They are wars for demonic strongholds to be defeated by the godly and righteous who pray and stand in faith and wait on their God to deliver them. Angelic hosts come and invade territories to bring assistance to those fighting on behalf of God Himself. Then the demonic is defeated and God can rule in the nations.

The great and final climax to this story is that now King Darius sees the goodness of God and wants to worship Daniel's God. The God Daniel serves is a living God. King Darius issues a proclamation to the people of his nation:

Then King Darius wrote to all the nations and peoples of every language in all the earth: "May you prosper greatly! I issue a decree that in every part of my kingdom people must fear and reverence the God of Daniel. For he is the living God and he endures forever; his kingdom will not be destroyed, his dominion will never end. He rescues and he saves; he performs signs and wonders in the heavens and on the earth. He has rescued Daniel from the power of the lions." So Daniel prospered during the reign of Darius and the reign of Cyrus the Persian (Daniel 6:25-28).

God's messengers do His bidding, and they came to Daniel's rescue and the impurities of the governmental kingdom were exposed. In this case, although I believe that Daniel's guardian angel was present, I believe that God called in seraphim and cherubim during this time simply because the issues were of a governmental nature and required a greater hierarchy of angelic hosts to release Daniel. When we pray for governments and nations, God will dispatch angels of fire because they have greater authority to carry the purifying fire of God to an impure nation.

One night at Freedom Destiny Church we had an encounter with a warrior angel of fire who came in and kneeled at the right side of our altar during worship. When I saw him, God said, "Pray now for the nation and call the church to pray for the pushing forward of votes being halted in our 2020 presidential election." This was the first time ever that our election was being held up with a final verdict of president not being announced on November 4, as the ballots were not being counted properly. We all interceded, and when we were finished declaring and decreeing then the angel got up and walked out the door. Our job as servants to the Lord was finished; the next day we heard officially that some of the states had finished counting. As the story goes, that was only the beginning of the ballot counting fraud and the governmental issues, but nonetheless, we and many others in the world were praying while angels were assisting in fighting the battle. This is an example of an angel visitation by a higher-ranking fire angel to bring purity to our nation. I am sure these angels visited many intercessors during that time.

When it comes to the exaltation of false gods over the Lord Himself, seraphim and cherubim are called in to bring fire from the altar and prepare other angels for this fight.

PRAYER FOR NATIONS

Let us take this time now to pray for nations and for governments.

Lord, I thank You for the angels of fire that are dispatched on behalf of nations to kill demonic giants and bring about Your will in the nations. We stand in the gap for nations now.

I want you to lift up the name of your nation. You may be in the United States, the United Kingdom, a European, African, North or South American, or Asian nation—any nation you are in, cry out to God now for corrupt governments to be taken down and enemy strongholds that do not serve and honor the one true living God to be demolished.

Lord, we thank You now for Your mercy. Send Your righteous fire to the earth, brought by the angels around Your fire altar. May we live to serve You and worship You only.

God, use me to pray for nations. I ask You for an anointing on my life to pray nations so I can help You bring Your righteousness and justice to the earth in the end-times. Thank You for Your Son, Jesus Christ, who makes a way for us to be righteous in Him. We stand in faith now for Your global glory and fire coming to the earth to purify us and make us whole. We love You and praise You, Lord Jesus!

CHAPTER 12

ANGELS OF PROVISION, PART 1

NGELS OF PROVISION OR REPLENISHMENT COME WHEN WE are in a place of deficit, lack, or poverty, but they are also present when God wants to take us to a new spiritual place of promotion. God will not take us to next levels without bringing forth provision for that next level of promotion. Our journey requires provision and replenishment so we do not run dry, but we have all we need and more than enough to get to where God is calling us. This was true for the Israelites in Exodus 23:20: "See, I am sending an angel ahead of you to guard you along the way and to bring you to the place I have prepared."

In this chapter, the Israelites are going to their promised land. The angel is a heavenly assigned escort for their journey. Some theologians say this angel is the Angel of the Lord, which is representative of Jesus Himself and this angel has characteristics of

Jehovah in that His name is in Him. God then goes on to list seven promised blessings He had for them. It was important for the Israelites to come from their place of slavery and the Egyptian life of lack and need, so God sent provision from heaven in the form of an angel to escort them to the land of milk and honey. God did not want them to turn back in fear. He made all provision for them to get there and not die doing it.

God is doing the same for you now. He is taking you to a place of promise and you have to make it—you cannot die getting there. God has a plan, purpose, destiny, and a place of promise for you and your gifts to be revealed in the earth, and an angel is assigned to get you to where God is calling you. This angel will bring you from a stagnant place or a lesser place to a place of more. This will be a place of increase for you, a place of destiny. This place has more than enough. But this place of provision needs a guide. We need an angel to bring us into the next-level assignments that God has for us.

THE PROMISES OF GOD

God says in Exodus 23:21, "Pay attention to him [the angel sent to guide them] and listen to what he says. Do not rebel against him; he will not forgive your rebellion, since my Name is in him." This angel is the first blessing of God. In verse 22, He adds, "If you listen carefully to what he says and do all that I say, I will be an enemy to your enemies and will oppose those who oppose you." This angel will be a source of protection that leads us to the place of promise and greater provision. In Exodus 23:25-26, the Lord speaks about the importance of worshiping Him and gives three more blessings:

> *Worship the Lord your God, and his blessing will be* **on your food and water***. I will* **take away sickness** *from among you, and none will miscarry or be barren in your land. I will give you* **a full life span**.

Then the Lord says in Exodus 23:29-30:

> *I will not drive them* [Israel's enemies] *out in a single year, because the land would become desolate and the wild animals too numerous for you. Little by little I will drive them out before you, until you have increased enough to take possession of the land.*

In other words, He will not give the whole promise to us in fullness until we have strengthened enough to take it completely. We must learn to exercise our faith and work with heaven to bring about the results on the earth and we will practice this more each year. The prosperity will come yearly! Yes, every year you will expand and grow more in your faith and more in understanding the supernatural. You will begin to walk out the blessing in the earth. We grow with God and the move of heaven on the earth and participation with the angels. Each year we can expect greater growth and greater understanding of heaven.

The final blessing is from Exodus 23:31: "I will establish your borders from the Red Sea to the Mediterranean Sea, and from the desert to the Euphrates River." The angel helped to strengthen them so they could take the new territory bit by bit until they had fought the enemies in the land and were able to manage the new territory.

Let me tell you these blessings are ours for every year. Every year we will rise to a new level of grabbing hold of the destiny before us. We will have a special blessing given to us at Passover time. This means greater connection with God and the angelic hosts. This angel assigned to us will reveal heavenly things because heaven is our home, and it is the promised land that we are called to live in fully now on earth.

Provisional increase comes first by faith and in the spirit realm. Then, when your soul grasps more of the revelation from heaven, you can walk in greater victory and take on more of the promise you were created for. Every year, expect these blessings to come to pass. Each year will bring us back to this place of promotion because Passover is a time of promotion in the spirit realms.

The New Year on the Hebrew calendar is in the month of Nissan, during Passover. Every year this month comes around, and God will send an angel to help bring you into that year's provisional increase. It was Passover when I encountered a new angel assigned to me at my time of yearly promotion.

A NEW ANGEL FOR PROMOTION

Each time God promotes me, He gives me an encounter with an angel. At Passover in 2020, God gave me an encounter in a dream with an angel named Mary Gold. This angel had gifts of healing and great power. She laid hands on me in my dream, and I felt this great power from heaven come into my body. My hands got fiery hot and the holiness of God surrounded me. I began to weep in the spirit, and God spoke to me about positional increase coming and told me that He had assigned a new angel to me to bring me into my promise. The angel's name was Mary Gold. Remember, angels are usually described as in a masculine tense, but this feminine tense is all I could say to describe this angel encounter.

Immediately, I felt the holiness of God. I began to confess sin, wanting to surrender all earthly positions and means of reaching goals on the earth. I confessed my ego, especially in the area of social media. For me, social media is how I communicate with most of those who follow the ministry, and I always want to see God expand social media to reach more people. It is not sin to want to expand the gospel, but it is sin if you ruminate on it, which is what happens sometimes when we are trying to expand our own territories, if you know what I mean. But it's amazing how the grace of God will cause us to confess sin.

> *The law was brought in so that the trespass might increase.*
> *But where sin increased, grace increased all the more, so*
> *that, just as sin reigned in death, so also grace might reign*
> *through righteousness to bring eternal life through Jesus*
> *Christ our Lord* (Romans 5:20-21).

After this encounter, I had to do some research about Mary Gold. She is a cherub angel of promotion and provision. God spoke to me that the angel represented the provision of gold. Gold is a precious metal that supersedes all other metals in its purity. It is highly valuable and stands in the heaven and earth realm as carrying more provision than other metals. This angel was assigned to me because God was bringing forth a fresh anointing of provision that was necessary for new territories I was going to enter into.

This angel also had access to the heavenly vats and could bring gold from the vats of heaven to the earth realm. In my book

Releasing Heaven, I speak of the vats of heaven and how they are open to us today. In Hosea 2:21-23, when Israel is being restored to relationship with God, the vats of heaven are opened:

> *"In that day I will respond," declares the Lord—"I will respond to the skies, and they will respond to the earth; and the earth will respond to the grain, the new wine and the olive oil, and they will respond to Jezreel. I will plant her for myself in the land; I will show my love to the one I called 'Not my loved one.' I will say to those called 'Not my people,' 'You are my people'; and they will say, 'You are my God.'"*

These vats are open to us now, but there are more vats than just oil, grain, and wine—there are also gold, silver, bronze, flax, and water. These are commodities held in the heavenly reserves for our use in the earth when we need them. God will assign an angel to you that will provide your needs on your journey.

ANGELS OF GOLD

In Revelation, when describing the new heaven and earth, it says, "The angel who talked with me had a measuring rod of gold to measure the city, its gates and its walls" (Rev. 21:15). Angels wear gold and they carry gold. In the endtimes, we see angels with gold as representatives that follow after the Lord and Savior Jesus Christ. The apostle John had this vision of Jesus wearing gold cloth:

> *There with the lampstands was someone who seemed to be the Son of Man. He was wearing a robe that reached down to his feet, and a gold cloth was wrapped around his chest* (Revelation 1:13).

Many objects at the Royal Table in heaven are gold, such as the lampstands, plates, dishes, utensils, and chalices. Many of these are listed in Exodus 25. Notice how Jesus is also revealed as "his eyes were like blazing fire. His feet were like bronze glowing in a furnace, and his voice was like the sound of rushing waters" (Rev. 1:14-15). Remember that the angels of fire carry the characteristics of the Lord.

We have more metals as part of the makeup of heaven, the throne room, and the angels, especially cherubim. Gold, silver, platinum, and palladium are called precious metals. Precious metals have great wealth and value in the earth and kingdom of heaven.

Angels and gold are common in heaven and they will be common in the new earth. Mary Gold is a carrier of provision into the earth realm. When I encountered her, my faith increased, and my finances in that season increased. I am still being challenged by the encounter, and God is continuing to reveal more to me about Mary Gold in the healing ministry.

It is good to know you have access to the vats of heaven because you are seated with Christ in heavenly places. The angels of provision are in the heavenly places and have the authority of heaven to bring you provision from these vats. Open your mind to receive. Let us pray for you to have an impartation of faith in this area:

Lord, thank You for assigning us angels to take us into the places of promise You have for us. Open our hearts to understand the gold angels of provision. We surrender our hearts and confess sin in any area so that You will reveal to us the angels paving the way for promotion in our lives. Keep our hearts and minds open and share with us and increase our faith and understanding in this area.

CHERUBIM LIKE GOLD

Let us learn some more about the cherubim, who can be depicted as fire angels of gold. They were in the Garden of Eden as guards:

So the Lord God banished him from the Garden of Eden to work the ground from which he had been taken. After he drove the man out, he placed on the east side of the Garden of Eden cherubim and a flaming sword flashing back and forth to guard the way to the tree of life (Genesis 3:23-24).

Only an angel that could withstand that kind of heat could guard a flaming sword. They have the power to guard areas of great flame without burning. Gold can withstand heat up to 1064 degrees. Gold also has a yellow-orange color to it, so cherubim are often seen as bright gold. Cherubim were present on the ark of the covenant in gold. Even though they were not real, their likeness was still a powerful representative.

Make an atonement cover of pure gold—two and a half cubits long and a cubit and a half wide. And make two cherubim out of hammered gold at the ends of the cover. Make one cherub on one end and the second cherub on the other; make the cherubim of one piece with the cover, at the two ends. The cherubim are to have their wings spread upward, overshadowing the cover with them. The cherubim are to face each other, looking toward the cover (Exodus 25:17-20).

In Exodus 36:8, they were placed on curtains to guard the tabernacle openings.

> *All those who were skilled among the workers made the tabernacle with ten curtains of finely twisted linen and blue, purple and scarlet yarn, with cherubim woven into them by expert hands.*

In the next few scriptures, God is enthroned between the cherubim, which are protecting and guarding Him.

> *And Hezekiah prayed to the Lord: "Lord, the God of Israel, enthroned between the cherubim, you alone are God over all the kingdoms of the earth. You have made heaven and earth"* (2 Kings 19:15).

> *Hear us, Shepherd of Israel, you who lead Joseph like a flock. You who sit enthroned between the cherubim, shine forth before Ephraim, Benjamin and Manasseh. Awaken your might; come and save us. Restore us, O God; make your face shine on us, that we may be saved* (Psalm 80:1-3).

> *Lord Almighty, the God of Israel, enthroned between the cherubim, you alone are God over all the kingdoms of the earth. You have made heaven and earth* (Isaiah 37:16).

PRAYER TO RELEASE VATS

Lord, I pray for my friend reading this today. Where there is doubt in their minds, remove it. Let them not get focused on the name of the angel Mary Gold but on what that angel represents, which is the purity of gold in heaven being released in the earth to those who are

Your children. We have every blessing for us in the spirit realms. Let us learn to navigate those blessings so we can realize them in the here and now in earth. By faith, Lord, open up the vats of heaven and release the gold and silver we need for the promise and destiny that You have called us to. Let all provision You have stored in heaven, bought by the sacrifice of Jesus, be ours today by faith. Thank You, Lord, for all You have done. I pray an impartation on my friend now to have the faith to release heavenly vats and to stand in the gap for their needs and the needs of others so that kingdom purpose can be made manifest in the earth realm today!

DECLARATIONS SEND ANGELS

God has set you apart for service unto His kingdom. He has assigned an angel to you from conception. We are called to declare and decree what heaven says on the earth. When we do this, angels will come and bring heaven to earth. How do we know this?

This, then, is how you should pray: "Our Father in heaven, hallowed be your name, your kingdom come, your will be done, on earth as it is in heaven" (Matthew 6:9-10).

It is God's will that heaven come to earth. Heaven comes to earth through us declaring and decreeing the will of God. We are God's voice pieces, His agents of change, working together with the angels to bring His plans into fruition on the earth.

Thou shalt also decree a thing, and it shall be established unto thee: and the light shall shine upon thy ways (Job 22:28 KJV).

When we stand in faith and make declarations and decrees from the Word of God, God begins to send angels to perform the fulfillment of the decree that was written in the scrolls of heaven.

You might say, "Well, I don't know what was written in the scrolls of heaven." Do you know the scrolls of heaven have our destinies written on them? I have seen the room in heaven with the scrolls. One day, I had an open vision of a library and a large desk. There was an angel in the room. I came to stand at the desk, and this huge angel with wings handed me a scroll. Behind him were tons of scrolls. This scroll was written about me, but also about many others who were in the room. I was being shown the room so I could see the importance to God of the fulfillment of our destiny and that of others. We have a mandate to fulfill our own destiny but also to stand in the gap for others' destinies to be fulfilled as well.

SCROLLS OF HEAVEN PRAYERS

In order to begin to grasp this revelation, simply begin to ask the Lord, "Lord, what has been written about me? What has been written about my purpose, my destiny?" Let Him know you want to fulfill what is written on the scroll about your life. You also want to know what has been written about your husband or your wife or your children so you can pray proper prayers.

God desires for you to know what's written in the scrolls, because when you know what's written in them, you'll stand firm

197

in understanding the will of God for your life and the will of God for your family's life. Then, as you began to pray and hold fast to that word, God will send the angels to come and perform it.

I can remember a time when I needed to see the scrolls in heaven for someone I loved very much. Their life did not look the way I believed was God's will. I began to start praying in tongues for hours. I became so entrenched with the situation because I really wanted to see things change. Finally I said, "God, I need to know what's written over this person's life. I need to agree with You on that. Lord, will You show that to me so that I can begin declaring and decreeing it? And then I know You're going to dispatch the angels to go and take care of this."

Sure enough, that's what I did. I declared what I believe I saw by faith. I decreed what the scrolls of heaven said as God began to reveal it to my heart. When I started standing firm in my heart and declaring and decreeing the things that I was hearing in my spirit about my family member, within 24 hours their life was dramatically turned around. I believe it was because I listened to the Lord and listened to things that were written in the scrolls of heaven.

Think for a moment—what has been spoken about you or about the loved one you are praying for? These things are good and beautiful things. There are things that God sees concerning your purpose, destiny, hope, and future. There are things to manifest the kingdom of God on earth through you.

When God revealed the scrolls, I heard good and purposeful things about this person even though their life wasn't looking like it. I held to the good, I spoke the good, and the angels were dispatched. In 24 hours, what was bad became lovely. I believed what God had spoken to my heart about the goodness of the person—not believing the bad, not believing the difficulty, but believing the good and the goodness of God and the goodness that He wanted to do in the earth. I just had to declare it. This is Romans 8:28 in action:

> *And we know that in all things God works for the good of those who love him, who have been called according to his purpose.*

FAITH CHALLENGE

I just want to challenge you right now. There are things that you feel in your heart about people, and you need to ask God for the truth. Say, "God, show me what is the truth about this person. What was written in the scrolls about them? Let me agree with You on that, God. Lord, I thank You that You're going to dispatch the angels because they hearken to the word that I'm going to speak over their life."

You may even be angry or frustrated with this person. Ask God for His heart for them and for what the scrolls say, not what your upset feelings say regarding this person. We must declare and decree from God's words and thoughts, not our own. If we harbor anger against people, it is hard to pray for them, and we may be the exact person God needs to pray for them, but we don't because of our bitterness or resentment. I am feeling someone is going to read this who knows they should be praying but they are not. If this is you, simply ask for forgiveness and say:

> *Lord, heal my heart of the anger or resentment I have toward _____ (write their name). I know I am equipped to intercede for them, but they have*

hurt me and I do not want to. Open my ears to hear You, Lord. Please forgive me as I know You want to use me to declare and decree life and destiny for them today. Open my heart, Lord, to Your heart for them, to hear the scrolls written for them so I can stand with You and heaven on their behalf.

Now, I believe God is going to use you! A change will be made and you can do this for husbands, wives, children, families, and friends. You can make the difference; you simply have to believe in your heart. God has spoken and written goodness about the people you love. Don't pay attention to feelings. What's in the scrolls is good, positive, hopeful, and a future. Begin to speak that, and the angels will come and hearken to that word over their life.

CHAPTER 13

ANGELS OF PROVISION, PART 2

G OD USES ANGELS FOR DIVINE TURNAROUNDS. GOD WILL TAKE bad things and use them for the good, as He says in Romans 8:28, "And we know that all things work together for good to them that love God, to them who are the called according to his purpose" (KJV). Angels are sent to make things lovely that are bad or difficult. God will send an angel on your behalf if you are stuck in a difficult situation as it is God's plan and purpose you be set free to continue to spread His love and the gospel.

PETER RELEASED BY ANGELS

The apostle Peter had a purpose and destiny on the earth, and God was not finished with him when he went to prison for his faith. God's plan was only beginning. Let's read about how the angels of provision had a role in Peter's life when he was imprisoned for his faith.

In Acts 12, Peter found himself being arrested and put in prison by King Herod for spreading the gospel. King Herod had James, the brother of John, put to death with the sword. When he saw that this met with approval among the Jewish leaders, he proceeded to seize Peter. This actually happened during Passover. Imagine that—a time of promotion in the spirit realm was a time when an angel was dispatched to help Peter fulfill his destiny.

> *After arresting him, he put him in prison, handing him over to be guarded by four squads of four soldiers each. Herod intended to bring him out for public trial after the Passover. So Peter was kept in prison,* **but the church was earnestly praying to God for him** (Acts 12:4-5).

It's really the last part that says it all: "The church was earnestly praying to God for him." Peter's in prison, but when the church starts praying, things start happening. That word *church* in Greek is *ekklesia*, which means the "called out ones." The ones with heavenly authority come and they start praying. Jesus had resurrected and ascended by this point and the church had too. Remember the ascension mind-set for a victorious church. The church prayed from their seat of authority in heaven. And what happened?

> *Suddenly an angel of the Lord appeared and a light shone in the cell. He struck Peter on the side and woke him up. "Quick, get up!" he said, and the chains fell off Peter's wrists* (Acts 12:7).

God's angels showed up suddenly in a bad situation. An angel turnaround was here! They released Peter from prison. They took a bad situation and made it lovely. So what's the key? Prayer from the ascension seat. You're a member of the church of Jesus Christ. You have upon you all the authority that's been given to you from the kingdom of God, which is the fullness of everything Jesus accomplished—His finished work. He died, was buried, resurrected, and ascended, and all that power is in your hands. All you have to do is pray, and God will send an angel to take your situation and make it right.

We pray in faith. Why? Because this is what the Word says. Peter was released from prison as the church was praying, so you too can be released from prison. Your family and friends can be released from prison. It may not be the bars of a natural prison cell. It may be the bondage of a spiritual prison that you're involved in, including depression, anxiety, heaviness, and generational sin— these kinds of things. When you start praying, God will send an angel to pull you out of the prison you're in and reposition you. The Word tells us in Acts 12:8-10:

> *Then the angel said to him, "Put on your clothes and sandals." And Peter did so. "Wrap your cloak around you and follow me," the angel told him. Peter followed him out of the prison, but he had no idea that what the angel was doing was really happening; he thought he was seeing a vision. They passed the first and second guards and came to the iron gate leading to the city. It opened for them by itself, and they went through it. When they had walked the length of one street, suddenly the angel left him.*

Peter followed the angel out of the prison, but he had no idea that this was really happening. He thought he might be seeing a vision. But the angel brought him out of the most difficult situation until the angel wasn't needed anymore. The angel gave specific instructions to Peter that came direct from the Lord, as angels hearken to the voice of the Lord. The angel would have heard God's voice say, "Go get my boy, Peter, out of prison, and this is what I need you to tell him to do." So the angel exactly followed the instructions that were given to him by the Lord. God is sending instructions to angels about you and your prison situation, your difficult situation, whatever it is.

I believe this angel was an angel of fire. This angel had governmental authority—it could break the chains of the government over Peter's life. It was sent as a result of the church praying, so the church was breaking governmental strongholds, which caused the release from the hierarchy. The power of church prayer broke a stronghold that released an angel with power and governmental authority to do this miracle.

I believe Peter's guardian angel was there too, and Peter could also have been seeing his guardian angel with delegated governmental authority. Guardian angels can have power delegated to them, by transference, to accomplish things that higher-level angels would usually take charge of.

ANGELS COLLECT PRAYERS

The Word says that the angels "were holding golden bowls full of incense, which are the prayers of God's people" (Rev. 5:8). Your prayers are going in a bowl. And after a while, they are going to be stirred up with the angels, and it's going to come right back down to earth and you're going to get your answer. With your answer will come a release for you, a release from prison. Not only will you be released, you'll also be replenished.

There are angels of provision and replenishment for you. There is an angel turnaround for you. I'm agreeing with you right now in the mighty name of Jesus. See, eventually your prayers, declares, and decrees come to the place where they are released from heaven into the earth.

Right now, I'm believing for a "suddenly" to happen in your life. I'm believing that while you're reading this right now, there's going to be a sudden angel turnaround, and you're going to get a retrieval. You're going to get a promotion away from your current situation and into a destiny move that will bring provision and replenishment. Something is going to happen! Those chains are going to break and you will step into that place of victory that you've been asking for!

Now, Peter thought he was having a vision, but it turned out to be a real, physical encounter. After he was released:

> *When this had dawned on him, he went to the house of Mary the mother of John, also called Mark, where many people had gathered and were praying. Peter knocked at the outer entrance, and a servant named Rhoda came to answer the door. When she recognized Peter's voice, she was so overjoyed she ran back without opening it and exclaimed, "Peter is at the door!" "You're out of your mind," they told her. When she kept insisting that it was so, they said, "It must be his angel" (Acts 12:12-15).*

I think this is really interesting. A real angel released Peter, and then Peter actually showed up in the flesh at the door and they thought they were seeing an angel. These people had faith! Angelic activity was normal for them. If it were not, they would not have thought Peter was an angel. This angel they thought they saw was in human form, not with wings. Remember Hebrews 13:2: "Do not forget to show hospitality to strangers, for by so doing some people have shown hospitality to angels without knowing it."

You could be entertaining angels in human form tonight at your dinner table. Peter was in the flesh and they called him an angel. You never know who you may encounter. I know that I have seen angels in the flesh before—one minute they're there and the next minute they're gone. When they come, they bring a blessing. Then you're like, "Where did they go?" You don't necessarily realize they're an angel at the beginning, but by the time they've gone, you're like, "Wow, I must have seen an angel." We need to have that level of faith. God wants us to be in that place.

HONOR GOD FOR ANGELIC ASSISTANCE

*But Peter kept on knocking, and when they opened the door and saw him, they were astonished. Peter motioned with his hand for them to be quiet and described how **the Lord** had brought him out of prison. "Tell James and the other brothers and sisters about this," he said, and then he left for another place* (Acts 12:16-17).

In this scripture, Peter gave glory to God for taking him out of prison. The angels don't want your glory. The angels exist for the glory of God. When an angel comes to bless you, bring you provision or replenishment, release you from prison, or do the miraculous, you are called to honor God for what His servants, the angels, have done at His command. You can thank your angel, and it's OK to praise God along with them, but it was the Father who released you. It was God who did the mighty work. It's very important that we understand this. We don't pray to angels. We pray to God, and then God sends an angel on our behalf. This is our security—our prayers go to heaven. Think of it this way—we as humans are the servants of the Lord. When we do something amazing, we recognize that God chose to use us miraculously, and God gets the glory. We get the joy of participating with Him, but He gets the glory.

> *Let us therefore come boldly unto the throne of grace, that we may obtain mercy, and find grace to help in time of need* (Hebrews 4:16 KJV).

We go to the throne room to receive grace, and part of that grace for us as His servants is an angel release. We enter and we ask God, and then He sends out the orders for the supernatural beings to be released. If you want to see the supernatural in your life, go to the throne room first. Better yet, keep your heavenly ascension mind-set and don't leave your righteous position in Christ in the first place. Then you will see angels being released on behalf of those in earth realm. Remember, your body is in the earth realm, but your spirit and soul should be taking its heavenly seat so you can activate things in the earth. I love how God comes to perform His Word. He wants us to use the Word and He performs it (see Jer. 1:12).

When the Word goes out, it does not return void. It accomplishes the purpose for which it has been sent (see Isa. 55:11). Go to the throne room, ask the Father, and He will release angels. I believe that as you are reading this now your faith is increasing, so I want you to just start praying for God to release angels in your life.

ANGELS PROTECT THE PROMOTED

The time of Passover, or the Feast of Unleavened Bread, is a miraculous time of angels being dispatched to bring us into destiny. Many times, we are launched into destiny after first facing a life-altering decision. We saw that with Peter and now with Jesus:

> *Jesus went out as usual to the Mount of Olives, and his disciples followed him. On reaching the place, he said to them, "Pray that you will not fall into temptation." He withdrew about a stone's throw beyond them, knelt down and prayed, "Father, if you are willing, take this cup from me; yet not my will, but yours be done." An angel from heaven appeared to him and strengthened him. And being in anguish, he prayed more earnestly, and his sweat was like drops of blood falling to the ground* (Luke 22:39-44).

In this passage, we see that in Jesus' most crucial time a servant God sent to strengthen Him for His destiny? It was an angel. You can be sure that when you are on the cusp of your destiny, God will dispatch an angel to bring you provision and replenishment for your promotion. Promotion may bring sorrow at first, but in your destined purpose it will bring forth joy in the end. That is what

Jesus' death, burial, and resurrection does for us. This was Jesus' promotion time. As He faced death, as a sheep to be slaughtered, angels were positioned to help bring God's plan and purpose to the earth. Jesus' death, burial, resurrection, and ascension were destiny for Him and ultimately for us, because we received life eternal.

In First Kings 19, we have another case of a man called by God who was in a place to realize his destiny. After his triumph at Mount Carmel, we find the prophet Elijah running from Jezebel:

> *Elijah was afraid and ran for his life. When he came to Beersheba in Judah, he left his servant there, while he himself went a day's journey into the wilderness. He came to a broom bush, sat down under it and prayed that he might die. "I have had enough, Lord," he said. "Take my life; I am no better than my ancestors." Then he lay down under the bush and fell asleep.*
>
> *All at once an angel touched him and said, "Get up and eat." He looked around, and there by his head was some bread baked over hot coals, and a jar of water. He ate and drank and then lay down again. The angel of the Lord came back a second time and touched him and said, "Get up and eat, for the journey is too much for you." So he got up and ate and drank. Strengthened by that food, he traveled forty days and forty nights until he reached Horeb, the mountain of God. There he went into a cave and spent the night* (1 Kings 19:3-9).

Doesn't this story look a lot like Jesus when He was in the Garden? Both of these men, called by God, fulfill their destiny at the end of their strength for their journey, and we find angels tending to them to bring provision and replenishment. I also find it interesting that in today's Passover seder meals in Judaism, Jewish families fill a cup with wine for Elijah, and it sits on the table untouched. They are waiting for the redemption of the Jews, when Elijah comes to drink of the cup with them. They believe when Elijah returns he will usher in the Messianic age. The Jews wait for their promotion during Passover.

Christians know the Messiah came in Jesus, the Passover Lamb who brought us from the slavery of sin to the restoration and fullness of eternal life in the Promised Land of heaven. The spirit of Elijah did return in John the Baptist, as stated by Jesus Himself in Matthew 11:13-15:

> For all the Prophets and the Law prophesied until John. And if you are willing to accept it, he is the Elijah who was to come. Whoever has ears, let them hear.

Why is this important? Both Jesus and Elijah were touched by angels who brought them replenishment. We also remember that God said, "For he will command his angels concerning you to guard you in all your ways; they will lift you up in their hands, so that you will not strike your foot against a stone" (Ps. 91:11-12). Angels will be sent to protect, provide, replenish, and carry His people to destiny. We see that in all the examples above. What message does this have for you?

God is no respecter of persons. What He has done for them He will do for you. When I was promoted, He sent me Yah-Red, Tracker Angel, and Mary Gold. He will send you the help you need just in time. He does this because your life has value and you mean so much to Him that He sent Jesus to die, be buried, resurrect, and ascend for you to have life. Jesus suffered and shed His blood so that we might be the recipients of this grace and love of God. God will never leave you or forsake you, and He will bring you into your promised land and destiny. He will use angels to do this for you by bringing provision, protection, replenishment, and all you need. Gold is on its way from the vats of heaven.

I feel that you are getting encouraged and grabbing hold by faith that you can stand on this same word given to Jesus, Elijah, and Peter, and God will rescue you. You can stand on Exodus 23:20, knowing God will bring you into your destiny.

DECLARATIONS FOR DESTINY

The angel of provision carries us to destiny. We know destiny is God's plan for His children. We were made to advance the kingdom of God. How do we do this? By having an angel assigned to us at conception. You are important to God and your children are important, and all of you carry forth the assignment He has given you in the earth realm. God has given you dominion over the earth, but you are not called to do it alone. You have been given guardian angels to watch over you and help you.

> *I declare and decree today the vats of heaven with grain, wine, oil, gold, silver, flax, water, and fire are coming down upon your life so that you will fulfill the reason you were created to live on this earth. I declare and decree the scrolls of heaven are fulfilled as angels come to your aid with provision and replenishment to your spirit, soul, and body. I declare and decree life over your soul and body,*

and you will live and fulfill your destiny. I declare and decree that where you put aside your dream it is now being birthed again in your heart and you can do it! I declare and decree an angel is dispatched to carry your dream to fulfillment like in Exodus 23:20. Rise up and start running, my friend—you are headed for your destiny.

CHAPTER 14

ANGELS OF REVIVAL
IN THE ENDTIMES

A s we prepare our hearts for the coming of the Lord, we need to understand some principles for end-time revival. Revival first starts with prayer:

> *If my people, which are called by my name, shall humble themselves, and pray, and seek my face, and turn from their wicked ways; then will I hear from heaven, and will forgive their sin, and will heal their land. Now mine eyes shall be open, and mine ears attent unto the prayer that is made in this place* (2 Chronicles 7:14-15 KJV).

Angels respond to the prayers of the *ekklesia*, the church of God that has governmental authority from God on the earth. When we pray, heaven moves and angels of fire are dispatched from the throne room of God. The angels receive the prayers of the people and help to distribute the answers from heaven back to the earth in the form of fire. These, I believe, are seraphim at work.

Revival comes when the fire of God comes to purify His people, who are ready to live as God has always desired them to live. He comes to bring purity and holiness to the earth. He comes to clean it up. We first cry out in repentance and humility asking God to deal with us.

> *When he opened the seventh seal, there was silence in heaven for about half an hour. And I saw the seven angels who stand before God, and seven trumpets were given to them. Another angel, who had a golden censer, came and stood at the altar. He was given much incense to offer,* **with the prayers of all God's people,** *on the golden altar in front of the throne.* **The smoke of the incense, together with the prayers of God's people, went up before God from the angel's hand. Then the angel took the censer, filled it with fire from the altar, and hurled it on the earth;** *and there came peals of thunder, rumblings, flashes of lightning and an earthquake* (Revelation 8:1-5).
>
> *However, if you suffer as a Christian, do not be ashamed, but praise God that you bear that name. For* **it is time for judgment to begin with God's household;** *and if it begins with us, what will the outcome be for those who do not obey the gospel of God? And, "If it is hard for the righteous to be saved, what will become of the ungodly and the sinner?" So then, those who suffer according to God's will should commit themselves to their faithful Creator and continue to do good* (1 Peter 4:16-19).

We must be willing to let God deal with us. Purity, holiness, and righteousness are character traits of God, and the seraphim and cherubim carry these attributes from His throne to purify His world as He sees fit. In all miracles and healings, there is an element of fire that comes forth through His Word. The angels are present when these things happen. Where He is, angels are. They reside with Him. They carry His fire, glory, love, justice, peace, protection, provision, restoration, purification, holiness, and righteousness. They are an extension of Him. They are servants that do His bidding.

> *The Lord has established his throne in heaven, and his kingdom rules over all. Praise the Lord, you his angels, you mighty ones who do his bidding, who obey his word. Praise the Lord, all his heavenly hosts, you his servants who do his will. Praise the Lord, all his works everywhere in his dominion* (Psalm 103:19-22).

So what do angels do? They accomplish God's purpose and they obey His Word. Even on earth, people in leadership have other people following them to do their bidding. Well, in heaven the angels do this for God. They are servant followers night and day, who act like Him and do as He does and says. They work alongside us when we do and say what is in the Word. You have fire angels with you right now to assist you in prayer and healing ministry, keeping you in a place of accessing heaven, and keeping you holy by touching you with the glory of God. All you have to do is speak the Word of God and they will obey and hearken to it. Praise the Lord!

THE CHURCH'S ROLE

Make every effort to live in peace with everyone and to be holy; without holiness no one will see the Lord. See to it that no one falls short of the grace of God and that no bitter root grows up to cause trouble and defile many (Hebrews 12:14-15).

Blessed are the pure in heart, for they will see God (Matthew 5:8).

This is who we are to be as His church in the endtimes. He is coming back to a church without spot or wrinkle. How can this be so? The apostle Paul teaches the church at Ephesus about the mystery of gospel using an earthly example of a husband and wife. Jesus is the head of the church, and we the church are His body. This reveals God's heart of how He loves and cares for His church:

For the husband is the head of the wife as Christ is the head of the church, his body, of which he is the Savior. Now as the church submits to Christ, so also wives should submit to their husbands in everything. Husbands, love your wives, just as Christ loved the church and gave himself up for her to make her holy, cleansing her by the washing with water through the word, and to present her to himself as a radiant church, without stain or wrinkle or any other blemish, but holy and blameless. In this same way, husbands ought to love their wives as their own bodies. He who loves his wife loves himself. After all, no one ever hated their own body, but they feed and care for their body, just as Christ does the church—for we are members of his body. "For this reason a man will leave his father and mother and be united to his wife, and the two will become one flesh." This is a profound mystery—but I am talking about Christ and the church. However, each one of you also must love his wife as he loves himself, and the wife must respect her husband (Ephesians 5:23-33).

We cannot be without spot or wrinkle until we take our proper position in Him. We must understand that Christ overcame sin, death, and the grave, and the ascension makes it possible for us to be seated with Him in heavenly places where every spiritual blessing is ours.

But because of his great love for us, God, who is rich in mercy, made us alive with Christ even when we were dead in transgressions—it is by grace you have been saved. And God raised us up with Christ and seated us with him in the heavenly realms in Christ Jesus, in order that in the coming ages he might show the incomparable riches of his grace, expressed in his kindness to us in Christ Jesus. For it is by grace you have been saved, through faith—and this is not from yourselves, it is the gift of God—not by works, so that no one can boast. For we are God's handiwork, created in Christ Jesus to do good works, which God prepared in advance for us to do (Ephesians 2:4-10).

This has been done already. When we the church begin to live like this, we will be holy and walk in power on the earth. Then the angelic hosts will join with us because our faith is in what God says about who we are, and we are not waiting only for His return but now ruling on His behalf as His kingdom leaders.

Therefore, with minds that are alert and fully sober, set your hope on the grace to be brought to you when Jesus Christ is revealed at his coming. As obedient children, do not conform to the evil desires you had when you lived in ignorance. But just as he who called you is holy, so be holy in all you do; for it is written: "Be holy, because I am holy." Since you call on a Father who judges each person's work impartially, live out your time as foreigners here in reverent fear. For you know that it was not with perishable things such as silver or gold that you were redeemed from the empty way of life handed down to you from your ancestors, but with the precious blood of Christ, a lamb without blemish or defect. He was chosen before the creation of the world, but was revealed in these last times for your sake. Through him you believe in God, who raised him from the dead and glorified him, and so your faith and hope are in God (1 Peter 1:13-21).

We are called to be different. You are living on earth from your heavenly seat and God sees you as holy and righteous. This is where we must be in these last days as heaven joins with us and we see angelic intervention like never before. If you want to see angels manifest themselves and feel God's presence and participate with angels, then you must be like them. They are holy and purified first and live in the throne of heaven. They did not need salvation, as they did not sin, but we do, and when we are redeemed we can live and work alongside them to bring God's will to earth. Hebrews 2:5-8 clearly states our position in Christ:

It is not to angels that he has subjected the world to come, about which we are speaking. But there is a place where someone has testified: "What is mankind that you are mindful of them, a son of man that you care for him? You made them a little lower than the angels; you crowned them with glory and honor and put everything under their feet." In putting everything under them, God left nothing that is not subject to them. Yet at present we do not see everything subject to them.

Even the angels are subject to us because they are the servants of the Lord. Our salvation has made us rulers with Christ and heirs of salvation so that we can partner with them.

ANGELS ARE HARVESTERS

In the endtimes, we partner with angels for the harvest, bringing in souls to the kingdom of God through prayers and following their lead.

The Son of Man will send out his angels, and they will weed out of his kingdom everything that causes sin and all who do evil (Matthew 13:41).

Angels are harvesters. They harvest the land for God. They harvest the good from the evil, and we can read that in scripture also:

*Then will appear the sign of the Son of Man in heaven. And then all the peoples of the earth will mourn when they see the Son of Man coming on the clouds of heaven, with power and great glory. And **he will send his angels*** *with a loud trumpet call, **and they will gather his elect** from the four winds, from one end of the heavens to the other* (Matthew 24:30-31).

Who's going to collect you and take you to heaven at the end? It's going to be the angels. This is the rapture of the church.

Jesus explained the end-time parable of the weeds in the fields. In this parable, we see that God is sending His angels to make the earth like heaven and removing that which is not like Him. The angels are the ones who are sent to bring in the harvest:

> *As the weeds are pulled up and burned in the fire, so it will be at the end of the age. The Son of Man will send out his angels, and they will weed out of his kingdom everything that causes sin and all who do evil. They will throw them into the blazing furnace, where there will be weeping and gnashing of teeth. Then the righteous will shine like the sun in the kingdom of their Father. Whoever has ears, let them hear* (Matthew 13:40-43).

The word *kingdom* in this parable is the Greek word *basileia*, which means "royalty, rule, or realm." The realm of God and His royalty has come, but even now we are helping to prepare this realm. We are living out the Word of God daily as righteous men and women who live the ascension life here on the earth. Jesus spoke of this truth:

> *Once again, the kingdom of heaven is like a net that was let down into the lake and caught all kinds of fish. When it was full, the fishermen pulled it up on the shore. Then they sat down and collected the good fish in baskets, but threw the bad away. This is how it will be at the end of the*

age. The angels will come and separate the wicked from the righteous and throw them into the blazing furnace, where there will be weeping and gnashing of teeth. "Have you understood all these things?" Jesus asked. "Yes," they replied. He said to them, "Therefore every teacher of the law who has become a disciple in the kingdom of heaven is like the owner of a house who brings out of his storeroom new treasures as well as old" (Matthew 13:47-52).

This means that those Jews who lived by the law and even taught by it who now received Jesus as Messiah would be storehouses of the power of the law and also the power of grace and the fulfillment of the times. Those teachers of the law would be carriers of a greater grace to those in the end times. It is like that with those of us who are growing in an awareness of the ascension life of the church. We are positioned not only with a knowledge of salvation but also a heavenly knowledge—a knowledge of living in earth with an ascension perspective. We are now the rulers who have dominion that will bring about what was prophesied by God:

So God created mankind in his own image, in the image of God he created them; male and female he created them. God blessed them and said to them, "Be fruitful and increase in number; fill the earth and subdue it. Rule over the fish in the sea and the birds in the sky and over every living creature that moves on the ground" (Genesis 1:27-28).

God has given us a mandate to do these five things: be fruitful, increase in number, fill the earth and subdue it, and rule or have dominion over it. As the church that has ascended with Christ,

221

we have this dominion and power just like Adam and Eve had in the garden. Jesus severed the stronghold of the enemy over us and then He positioned us to be seated with Him in heavenly places as an ascension church so we can rule and reign on the earth now in His power with the angels by our side. It is true that He will come back with His angels and an end-time reaping will occur, but we are called *now* to live like this in faith and not to wait.

> *For the Lord himself will come down from heaven, with a loud command, with the voice of the archangel and with the trumpet call of God, and the dead in Christ will rise first. After that, we who are still alive and are left will be caught up together with them in the clouds to meet the Lord in the air. And so we will be with the Lord forever. Therefore encourage one another with these words* (1 Thessalonians 4:16-18).

There is a time coming when the church will be caught up to heaven with the voice of an archangel and a trumpet call, but until then we are called to act like we are risen now. When we do this, the angelic hosts cohabitate with us and do the work of the kingdom on earth now.

The angels watch our moves of faith and rejoice and follow the heirs of salvation as they live out now the ascension because of the resurrection. We have this power in earthen vessels:

> *But we have this treasure in earthen vessels, that the excellency of the power may be of God, and not of us. We are troubled on every side, yet not distressed; we are perplexed, but not in despair; persecuted, but not forsaken; cast down, but not destroyed; always bearing*

about in the body the dying of the Lord Jesus, that the life also of Jesus might be made manifest in our body. For we which live are always delivered unto death for Jesus' sake, that the life also of Jesus might be made manifest in our mortal flesh. So then death worketh in us, but life in you. We having the same spirit of faith, according as it is written, I believed, and therefore have I spoken; we also believe, and therefore speak; knowing that he which raised up the Lord Jesus shall raise up us also by Jesus, and shall present us with you. For all things are for your sakes, that the abundant grace might through the thanksgiving of many redound to the glory of God. For which cause we faint not; but though our outward man perish, yet the inward man is renewed day by day. For our light affliction, which is but for a moment, worketh for us a far more exceeding and eternal weight of glory; while we look not at the things which are seen, but at the things which are not seen: for the things which are seen are temporal; but the things which are not seen are eternal (2 Corinthians 4:7-18 KJV).

We are eternal creatures living in earth suits required to act heavenly even though we feel earthly. When we do this, all of heaven rejoices with us as we act in faith on what Jesus did and we begin to see miracles happen and angelic activity occur.

This life is for you now! Just begin to live and believe it as a citizen of the kingdom wearing His robe of righteousness and you will begin to attract angels to your atmosphere and sphere of influence.

ANGELS ARE WATCHFUL

When we are considering the return of Jesus, we must be watchful. Christ and the angels do not know the day or hour of Christ's return; however, they are watchful. We are called to create a heavenly habitation of watchfulness on the earth.

> *But about that day or hour no one knows, not even the angels in heaven, nor the Son, but only the Father. As it was in the days of Noah, so it will be at the coming of the Son of Man. For in the days before the flood, people were eating and drinking, marrying and giving in marriage, up to the day Noah entered the ark; and they knew nothing about what would happen until the flood came and took them all away. That is how it will be at the coming of the Son of Man. Two men will be in the field; one will be taken and the other left. Two women will be grinding with a hand mill; one will be taken and the other left. Therefore keep watch, because you do not know on what day your Lord will come* (Matthew 24:36-42).

In the very next chapter of Matthew, Jesus continues to emphasize this point in the parable of the ten virgins:

> *At that time the kingdom of heaven will be like ten virgins who took their lamps and went out to meet the bridegroom. Five of them were foolish and five were wise. The foolish ones took their lamps but did not take any oil with them. The wise ones, however, took oil in jars along with their lamps. The bridegroom was a long time in coming, and they all became drowsy and fell asleep. At midnight the cry rang out: "Here's the bridegroom! Come out to*

meet him!" Then all the virgins woke up and trimmed their lamps. The foolish ones said to the wise, "Give us some of your oil; our lamps are going out." "No," they replied, "there may not be enough for both us and you. Instead, go to those who sell oil and buy some for yourselves." But while they were on their way to buy the oil, the bridegroom arrived. The virgins who were ready went in with him to the wedding banquet. And the door was shut. Later the others also came. "Lord, Lord," they said, "open the door for us!" But he replied, "Truly I tell you, I don't know you." Therefore keep watch, because you do not know the day or the hour (Matthew 25:11-13).

We make ourselves ready by prayer and spending time in the presence of the Lord, activating our senses to the times and seasons and creating environments where angels can work alongside us to get things ready for the day and hour He comes. Heaven is waiting for the king to rule earth in person. We must wait and watch along with heaven and prepare this place as though He were here already. Angels prepare a place for Jesus, and we as the heirs of salvation are called to also. Angels will join us when we live by faith. We should be so eager for His return that we live like we're in heaven now, and we participate with angels now, and we seek His heart now on earth.

The Father is pleased when we operate in faith for what is to come and live it out now. We should be saturating ourselves in His presence and creating environments for angels, and then we will see heaven open and the Son of Man, Jesus, coming even now before He comes.

When I teach people these truths they begin to see and experience heaven. Their soul—their mind, will, and emotions—along with their spirit begin to grasp the reality that is before them, and they learn to live in that heavenly seat and begin to see earth responding.

There are many end-time scriptures where angels are present. As you can see from this whole book, there is a correlation between angels and fire. Angels and fire are compatible and both represent purity and holiness. In each case, angels are serving the King. They are where He is! And they are where we are because we are in Him.

The final end-time statement that Jesus makes is in Matthew 25:31-33, where He talks about separating the sheep from the goats. This is a judgment for those who believe and follow Him and those who do not. The angels of fire will play a role in His return and in this judgment. They accompany Him, as He is the head of the angel armies.

> *When the Son of Man comes in his glory, and all the angels with him, he will sit on his glorious throne. All the nations will be gathered before him, and he will separate the people one from another as a shepherd separates the sheep from the goats. He will put the sheep on his right and the goats on his left* (Matthew 25:31-33).

This is His second coming, when He declares Himself Lord of the earth. What category will you be in? Are you a sheep or a goat? Are you in a sheep nation that has claimed Jesus as Lord and Savior, or are you in a goat nation that does not believe He is the Savior of the world? It is time for us to decide where we are now.

If you are not a sheep, then it is time to repent. If you say you do not believe, you are part of the goats. He will take His sheep to their pasture of paradise, but the goats will be separated to a place of no rest. This place is called hell, and it is not for us. It was made for the fallen angels of destruction led by the forces of satan.

It is not too late to receive Jesus as your Lord and Savior if you have not. I have shared with you multiple times in this book the importance of repentance and purification of your heart. The angels carry fire from His altar to those He purifies for His kingdom. If you have repented before, you do not need to do this again. However, if you have not, here is another opportunity. All you have to do is believe in your heart and confess with your mouth Jesus as your Lord and Savior.

> *If you declare with your mouth, "Jesus is Lord," and believe in your heart that God raised him from the dead, you will be saved. For it is with your heart that you believe and are justified, and it is with your mouth that you profess your faith and are saved. As Scripture says, "Anyone who believes in him will never be put to shame." For there is no difference between Jew and Gentile—the same Lord is Lord of all and richly blesses all who call on him, for, "Everyone who calls on the name of the Lord will be saved"* (Romans 10:9-13).

PRAYER FOR SALVATION

If you want to do this now, simply say:

> *Father, forgive me of my sins. I have made mistakes; I have fallen short of the glory of God. I ask You to forgive*

me and cleanse my heart. I thank You for sending Jesus Christ, Your only begotten Son, to die on the cross for me, be buried, and resurrect so that I may be saved in my spirit and soul. I want to receive Jesus now as my Lord and Savior. I want You to come into my heart and make residency here. I want to live my life for You, Jesus, and make You Lord of my life. Thank You, Lord, for having mercy on me and I am grateful for Your righteousness and peace in my life.

If you just prayed this prayer, the Word says you are now saved and will spend eternity in the kingdom of heaven with Jesus. You are now a sheep in His paradise pasture.

Now call up someone and tell them the good news! It is time to celebrate! You are now an heir of salvation and you are seated with Christ in heavenly places. You are now a participator with the angels of fire in the endtimes. God is so good and He loves you so much! Your next step is to ask Him for the baptism of the Holy Spirit by fire. Just read Acts 2 about the tongues of fire and begin to pray. You are clearly on your way to being a living epistle to the love of Jesus. You are now a ruler in His kingdom and the angels will be working alongside you. I am so excited for you. Please reach out to me by email at info@candicesmithyman.com and tell me you received Jesus and I will send you a *free* gift.

FINAL PRAYER OF THANKSGIVING FOR ANGELS OF FIRE

Father, we give You glory, honor, praise, and thanksgiving for our angels of fire. We thank You that they do Your bidding. We thank You that they're messengers of Yours, Father, that sit in the throne room and know and understand the characteristics and the nature of God. We praise You and thank You, Father, that we are on the receiving end of that. Help us Lord Jesus to understand more who You are and the created beings that You've sent forth in the angels. We seek Your face. We worship You only. We do not worship angels. We pray to You only, Father, and we give You glory, honor, praise, and thanksgiving. Thank You, Jesus, for Your death, burial, resurrection, and ascension, which position us to be seated with You in heavenly places. This position means we have our eyes opened from heavenly places to be able to receive all that You want to give us, Father. We thank You, Lord Jesus, for the guardian angels that You have assigned to us to help us fulfill the assignments that You've given us on the earth. We thank You for equipping us to work and participate together with angels of fire for the kingdom of God in Jesus' name. We ask for more supernatural encounters as they share with us who You are and give us understanding about the heavenly place You are calling us to live from in these endtimes. Our sight, hearing, smell, taste, and touch are open to keep learning in the spirit realms until we are fully seated with You, not only in spirit and soul but in body too. Give us wisdom in these endtimes as Your church, which has the power and authority of the King on the earth. Let us stand for righteousness, peace, and justice as You do. We love You. Amen!

ANGELS OF FIRE HEALING CHART

HIERARCHY OF FIRE ANGELS (CALLED "FIRE ANGELS" BECAUSE THEY ALL CONNECT WITH THE THRONE OF GOD)

Archangels: silvery blue-white flames, head of legions—near to God

Seraphim: blue-white, also silvery (glory flames), some with orange, yellow, red—near to God

Cherubim: gold or amber with orange, yellow, red—near to God

Guardian angels: orange, yellow, red—nearer to us

All seraphim and cherubim fire angels bring sulfate from the throne room of God in the form of purifying coals from the throne just like in Isaiah 6:1-7.

When these mineral deficiencies of copper, calcium, sodium, lithium, and strontium are present, these angels bring these mineral properties from the throne of God.

BLUE FIRE ANGELS (SERAPHIM): COPPER SULFATE

Heal immune systems

Kill algae and fungus

Heart disease

Pale skin

Premature aging of hair

Bones—osteoporosis

Nerves

Blood vessels

Fatigue—low energy

Too much zinc

Needs more iron

Anemia

Low white blood cells

Celiac disease

Angels around throne are either seraphim or cherubim with the properties of heaven and they carry either silver with yellow, orange, red, *or* gold with yellow, orange, red.

- Seraphim: blue/silver-white hue
- Cherubim: gold/amber

YELLOW FIRE ANGELS (SERAPHIM/ CHERUBIM): SODIUM SULFATE

Heal muscles

Nerves

Balance body fluids

Increase pH balance

Fatigue

Headaches

Muscle cramps

Nausea

Irritability

Liver

Pancreas

Intestines

Kidneys

Influenza

Common colds

Stops bacteria growth

Acne

Rosacea

Seborrheic dermatitis

Works with potassium/magnesium

Addison disease

Low blood pressure to raise it

ORANGE FIRE ANGELS (SERAPHIM/ CHERUBIM): CALCIUM SULFATE

Bones

Teeth

Osteoporosis

Acne

Abscess

Ulcers

Wounds

Infected sores

Sore throat

Numbness in arms and legs

Dizziness, brain fog

Premenstrual syndrome

Depression

Chest pains

Cataracts

Seizures

RED FIRE ANGELS (SERAPHIM/CHERUBIM): LITHIUM AND STRONTIUM SULFATE

Lithium

An original element in the earth like hydrogen or helium.

Mental health

Autism

Bipolar

Depression

Anxiety

Excessive mood disorders

Strontium

Much like calcium in the body.

GREEN FIRE ANGELS (SERAPHIM/ CHERUBIM): BARIUM SULFATE

This mineral is found in soil and seawater; used in X-rays to see within body. These angels travel with red and blue fire angels as they assist them.

Digestive disorders

Esophagus

Stomach

Intestines

PURPLE FIRE ANGELS (SERAPHIM/ CHERUBIM): COPPER AND STRONTIUM

Heal immune systems

Kill algae and fungus

Heart disease

Pale skin

Premature aging of hair

Bones

Nerves

Blood vessels

Bones

Teeth

Osteoporosis

Acne

Abscess

Ulcers

Wounds

Infected sores

Sore throat

WHITE FIRE ANGELS (GLORY FLAME)

Type of seraphim: red, blue, and green hues working together make a white glow—can be referred to as *glory flame angels.*

About Candice Smithyman

Dr. Candice Smithyman is an apostolic and prophetic minister who is a founder and executive pastor of Freedom Destiny Church and founder of Dream Mentors International, a biblical and transformational life coaching school. She hosts the *Glory Road* television show on Faith Networks and various internet outlets. She also hosts *Your Path to Destiny* on Sid Roth's It's Supernatural Network. She has authored many books and writes for online publications like *Elijah List, Charisma,* and *Spirit Fuel.*